JUST PLAIN
DATA ANALYSIS

JUST PLAIN DATA ANALYSIS

Finding, Presenting, and Interpreting Social Science Data

Gary M. Klass

ROWMAN & LITTLEFIELD PUBLISHERS, INC.
Lanham • Boulder • New York • Toronto • Plymouth, UK

ROWMAN & LITTLEFIELD PUBLISHERS, INC.

Published in the United States of America
by Rowman & Littlefield Publishers, Inc.
A wholly owned subsidary of The Rowman & Littlefield Publishing Group, Inc.
4501 Forbes Boulevard, Suite 200, Lanham, Maryland 20706
www.rowmanlittlefield.com

Estover Road
Plymouth PL6 7PY
United Kingdom

British Library Cataloguing in Publication Information Available

Library of Congress Cataloging-in-Publication Data

Klass, Gary M., 1952–
  Just plain data analysis : finding, presenting, and interpreting social science data /
Gary M. Klass.
    p. cm.
  Includes bibliographical references.
  ISBN-13: 978-0-7425-6052-9 (cloth : alk. paper)
  ISBN-10: 0-7425-6052-X (cloth : alk. paper)
  ISBN-13: 978-0-7425-6053-6 (pbk. : alk. paper)
  ISBN-10: 0-7425-6053-8 (pbk. : alk. paper)
  1. Statistics. 2. Social sciences—Statistics. I. Title.
HA29.K58 2008
519.5—dc22   2007048770

Printed in the United States of America

∞™ The paper used in this publication meets the minimum requirements of American
National Standard for Information Sciences—Permanence of Paper for Printed Library
Materials, ANSI/NISO Z39.48-1992.

To the thousands of Illinois State and Illinois Wesleyan University students who have spent their Saturday mornings building thirteen Habitat for Humanity homes since 1995, and to Sarah and Trisha Klass.

Contents

List of Figures

List of Tables

Preface

What Is Just Plain Data Analysis?

"JUST PLAIN DATA ANALYSIS" IS, simply, compiling, evaluating, and presenting numerical evidence to support and illustrate arguments about politics and public affairs.

There is a realm of public debate about society's most contentious issues where arguments are grounded in hard evidence and sound reasoning. Often this evidence comes in the form of numerical measures of social conditions and of the effectiveness of public policies and governing institutions. When contending sides advance their causes by finding, presenting, and interpreting such evidence with clear thinking, the quality of public debate and the chances of devising effective solutions to society's problems are greatly increased.

The contending sides in such debate are rarely dispassionate and often present misleading evidence and deceptive reasoning, but the shortcomings of such arguments are transparent to those who can apply critical thinking skills to the evidence. This is often not the case in other realms of public debate, prevalent in today's broadcast media and, increasingly, in academic discourse, where competing anecdotes and malign characterizations of the other sides' motives are all too common.

Just plain data analysis is the most common form of quantitative social science methodology, although the statistical literacy skills and knowledge it entails are often not presented, or presented well, in social science research methods and statistics textbooks. These skills involve finding, presenting, and

interpreting numerical information in the form of commonly used social, political, and economic indicators. They are practical skills that students will
find they can readily apply in both in their subsequent coursework and in
their future careers.

Just plain data analysis differs from what is commonly regarded as quantitative social science methodology in that it usually does not involve formal
tests of theories, hypotheses, or null hypotheses. Rather than relying on statistical analysis of a single dataset, just plain data analysis, at its best, involves
compiling and evaluating all the relevant evidence from multiple data sources.
Where conventional approaches to quantitative social science analysis stress
the statistical analysis of data to model and test narrowly defined theories, just
plain data analysis stresses presenting and critically evaluating statistical data
to support arguments about social and political phenomenon.

Good examples of just plain data analysis are found in many books that advance comprehensive and data-based arguments about social issues written by
public intellectuals for a broad public audience. Often these works shape public debate about critical public policy issues. Charles Murray's 1984 book, *Losing Ground*, for example, presented evidence of rising welfare caseloads and
spending, undiminished poverty, and the breakdown of the two-parent family, which shaped conservative attacks on American welfare programs and
eventually led to the dramatic welfare reform policies during the Clinton administration.[1] Employing much of the same method of analysis, Jeffrey
Sachs's *The End of Poverty*, coming from a decidedly different ideological perspective, addresses issues of global poverty and may serve much the same role
in spurring progressive solutions to the intractable poverty of developing nations.[2]

At times both sides of a public debate use the same evidence to draw different conclusions. Thus, the annual *State of the World*[3] report, published by
the environmentalist organization of the Worldwatch Institute, regularly describes the deterioration of the world's environment on a wide range of ecological indicators. Bjorn Lomborg's critique of that report in *The Skeptical Environmentalist*[4] counters with evidence that long-term trends in deforestation
and in food, energy, and raw material production generally do not support the
environmentalists' dire predictions.

In *The Politics of Rich and Poor*, historian Kevin Phillips argued that the
Reagan administration policies were producing a new era of accelerating con-
centration of wealth, paralleling that of the Gilded Age and the Roaring Twen-
ties. In tables and charts, Phillips presents statistic after statistic demonstrat-
ing that the United States has the highest inequalities of wealth and income in
the developed world, the inequalities of wealth and income are steadily increasing, the divergence in pay for corporation executives and their employees

is widening, and the rich are much richer and the poor and middle class poorer.[5] The theme, using the same Gilded Age metaphor and fifteen more years of evidence, is repeated with fewer tables and no charts, but often with a much more careful analysis of the statistical evidence, in Paul Krugman's recent book, *The Conscience of a Liberal.*[6]

Robert Putnam's *Bowling Alone*, arguing that America faces a critical decline in social capital, is a classic example of just plain data analysis. Almost all of Putnam's analysis is grounded in quantitative data, from a wide variety of sources, presented in charts and graphs. Putnam describes his strategy as attempting to "triangulate among as many independent sources of information as possible" based on the "core principle" that "no single source of data is flawless, but the more numerous and diverse the sources, the less likely that they could all be influenced by the same flaw."[7] Legions of social scientists have applied Putnam's core ideas to many fields of scholarly research and public officials regularly cite his work in advancing new approaches to public issues.

Works such as these, and others addressing policy issues as diverse as gun control, the death penalty, racial and gender discrimination, national health care, school vouchers, and immigration, advance the argument on one side of the public debate and often set the research agenda for additional social science research.

Finding, Presenting, and Interpreting the Data

There are three tasks and skills involved in doing just plain data analysis that traditional research methods courses and textbooks often neglect: finding, presenting, and interpreting numerical evidence.

Finding the Data

With the advances in information technology over the past decade, there has been a revolution in the amount and availability of statistical indicators provided by governments and nongovernmental public and private organizations. In addition to the volumes of data provided by the U.S. Census Bureau, many federal departments now have their own statistics agency, such as the National Center for Education Statistics, the Bureau of Justice Statistics, the National Center for Health Statistics, the Bureau of Labor Statistics, and the Bureau of Transportation Statistics, providing convenient online access to comprehensive data collections and statistical reports. In recent years, the greatest growth in the shear quantity of statistical indicators has been in the field of education. The mandated testing under the No Child Left Behind law and the expansion of the Department of Education's National Assessment of Educational Progress have produced massive databases of measures of the performance of the nation's schools that, for better or worse, fundamentally transformed the administration of educational institutions.

There has also been significant growth in the quantity and quality of comparative international data. The Organisation for Economic Co-operation and Development (OECD) now provides a comprehensive range of governmental, social, and economic data for developed nations. For developing nations, the World Bank's development of poverty indicators and measures of business and economic conditions and the United Nations' Millennium Development Goals database have contributed greatly to public debate and analysis of national and international policies affecting impoverished people across the world. With the *Trends in International Math and Science Study* (TIMSS) and the *Programme in International Student Assessment* (PISA) both having completed multiyear international educational achievement testing, rich databases of educational system conditions and student performance are now easily accessible.

Similar growth has taken place in the availability of social indicator data derived from nongovernmental public opinion surveys that offer consistent times series and cross-national measures of public attitudes and social behaviors. Time series indicators can be readily obtained online from the U.S. National Elections Study and the National Opinion Research Center's annual General Social Survey and comparative cross-national data indicators can be accessed from Comparative Study of Electoral Systems, the International Social Survey Programme, and World Values Survey.

Finding the best data relevant to the analysis of contemporary social and political issues requires a basic familiarity with the kinds of data likely to be available from these sources. Social science research methods courses often give short shrift to this crucial stage of the research process that involves skills and expertise usually acquired by years of experience in specific fields of study. Too often, the data are a "given": the instructor gives a dataset to the students and asks them to analyze it. The concluding chapter of this book addresses the topic in some detail, but finding the best data is the subtext for all of the chapters and the examples and illustrations that follow.

Presenting the Data

Good data presentation skills are to data-based analysis what good writing is to literature, and some of the same basic principles apply to both. More important, poor graphical and tabular presentations often lead both readers and writers to draw erroneous conclusions from their data and obscure facts that better presentations would reveal. Some of these practices involve deliberate distortions of data, but more commonly they involve either unintentional distortions or simply ineffective approaches to presenting numerical evidence.

The past two decades have seen the development of a substantial literature on the art and science of data presentation, much of it following Edward R. Tufte's pathbreaking work, *The Visual Display of Quantitative Information*.[8] With his admonitions to "show the data," "minimize the ink-to-data ratio," and avoid "ChartJunk," Tufte established many of the basic rules and principles of data presentation and demonstrates over and over again how effective data presentations combined with clear thinking can reveal truths hidden in the data. Howard Wainer's work extends Tufte's standards and demonstrates the many errors that have ensued from statistical fallacies and faulty tabular and graphic design.[9] Few research methods and statistics texts address these standards of data presentation in more than a cursory manner and many demonstrate some of the worst data presentation practices.

Although the development of spreadsheet and other software has greatly simplified the tasks of tabular and graphical data presentation, it has also greatly facilitated some very bad data presentation practices.

Interpreting the Data

Good data analysis entails little more than finding the best data relevant to a given research questions, making meaningful comparisons among the data, and drawing sound conclusions from the comparisons. To evaluate arguments based on numerical evidence, one must assess the reliability and validity of the individual measures used and validity of conclusions drawn from comparisons of the data.

Assessing the reliability and validity of social indicator measurements requires that one understand how the data are collected and how the indicators are constructed. Many research methods and statistics texts address issues of measurement merely as matters of choosing the appropriate level of measurement for variables (nominal, ordinal, or interval) and of calculating sampling error. As a practical matter, such issues are usually irrelevant or trivial when one undertakes just plain data analysis. With just plain data analysis, almost all of the data are interval measures, in the form of ratios, percentages, and means, even if the base question for the indicator is nominal or ordinal. Measures of sampling error usually constitute the least important aspect of measurement reliability. In chapter 1 we will see that the least reliable measures of crime rates, based on the FBI Uniform Crime reports, have far less sampling error (actually no sampling error) than the more reliable measures based on the National Crime Victimization Surveys. The same thing occurs with the measurement of educational achievement discussed in chapter 5: the No Child Left Behind tests of all students are shown to be less reliable than the National Assessment of Education Progress tests based on national samples of students. Although assessing sampling error sometimes has a crucial role in some data analysis, in both academic research and news reporting the emphasis on sampling error often conveys a false sense of the reliability of data and distracts attention from more serious measurement problems.

Although some social scientists refrain from using the word "causation," the substantive import of most data analysis of any kind is that it provides evidence from which we can conclude that something causes something else. Chapter 1 presents the basic framework for drawing causal conclusions of numerical comparisons: one can be confident that an observed relationship is a causal relationship if one can reasonably conclude that alternative explanations for the relationship do not withstand scrutiny. It stresses that avoiding logical fallacies, rather than avoiding violations of statistical assumptions, is the key to not drawing false causal conclusions from the analysis of one's data. Just plain data analysis will never offer a definitive proof of casual claims, but nor will it pretend to.

Why We Should Teach Just Plain Data Analysis

Often a fear of mathematics, combined with nonsequential curricular requirements, leads students to take a research methods and statistics course only in their last semester of study. In departments that require freshmen to take introductory methods courses, the required course is often the last time in students' academic careers that they will actually do the quantitative analysis that is taught. It may even be the last time they will have to read research employing the methods that are taught.

Just plain data analysis involves skills and expertise that students can readily apply to the analysis of evidence presented in their course literature and in conducting their own research for term papers and independent study projects. Moreover, the data analysis and data presentation skills described here have widespread application in a wide range of future careers in both government and the private sector. It is a primary mode of communication in government and is found in the studies, annual reports, and PowerPoint presentations of almost every governmental agency and advocacy group or in any career that requires writing clearly and succinctly with numbers. It is not too late to read this text in the last semester of your senior year of college, but it is later than it should have been.

For departments that offer courses in both quantitative and qualitative methodology, just plain data analysis fills the methodological chasm that divides the social sciences. Those students who will go on to learn and apply the knowledge of the central limit theorem, multiple regression, factor analysis, and other less-plain statistical applications will discover that many of the principles of just plain data analysis will greatly improve the quality of the work. Those who embrace qualitative analysis out of bewilderment at the often tortuous mathematical complexities of contemporary quantitative social science may find less madness in the methods presented here. Students in almost every field of study encounter just plain data analysis all the time in the charts and tables presented in their textbooks.

In today's world the exercise of effective citizenship increasingly requires a public competent to evaluate arguments grounded in numerical evidence. As the role of government has expanded to affect almost every aspect of people's daily lives, the role of statistics in shaping governmental policies has expanded as well. To the extent the public lacks the skills to critically evaluate the statistical analyses that shape public policy, more crucial decisions that affect our daily lives will be made by technocrats who have these statistical skills or by those who would use their mastery of these skills to serve their own partisan or special interest ends.

Organization of This Book

Although the logic ordering of doing just plain data analysis is to find, present, and then interpret the data, it makes sense to cover these topics in reverse order. Finding the data and constructing a data presentation presupposes an understanding of how the data are going to be interpreted. Chapter 1 begins by stressing that an understanding of how social indicators are produced and constructed is fundamental to every other aspect of the data analysis. It then addresses data interpretation: how to assess the reliability and validity of the indicators and how to draw sound causal conclusions from data comparisons.

Chapters 2 and 3 illustrate the basic principles of the art and science of presenting numerical information in tables and charts and contain several examples of bad tabular and graphic design. What follow are three chapters applying and illustrating the principles of the first three chapters in more detail, focusing on the topics of voting, education, and poverty. Each of these chapters begins with a discussion of comparative international statistical measures, followed by U.S. data, and ends with an evaluation of specific examples of data-based arguments.

The last chapter serves as a general guide to finding international and U.S. national social indicator data and contains a discussion of the data sources used throughout the book.

A companion website (lilt.ilstu.edu/JPDA) for this text contains hyperlinks to all the spreadsheet files used to construct the tables and charts, the original data sources, and the other data sources listed in chapter 7. All of the charts prepared for this book were constructed with the 2007 version of Microsoft Excel® charting software, although some of the charts, particularly the box-plots and the data labels shown on the scatterplots, required the use of free, downloadable add-ins. The companion website contains links to those add-ins and instructions, tips, and tricks for using Excel to do the things demonstrated in the book.

Acknowledgments

The starting point for this book was a research methods course I taught to political science students at Binghamton University at a time when analyzing data required the use of keypunch and punch-card counter sorter machines. I have taught the methods course many times since, each time adding more of the practical data analysis material presented in this book. From the students in these courses, I have learned what they find most perplexing and challenging about numbers, and they have challenged me to find better ways of presenting this material. Working on their "data profile" term papers, many students discovered datasets and data sources that I was not familiar with and that are cited throughout this book. Three students in my Quantitative Reasoning course contributed more directly: Molly Miles and Shannon Durocher found several errors in a late draft of the book, and Lesley Clements contributed the first draft of the chart shown in figure 3.12.

To prepare the tables and charts in this book, I acquired near mastery of the 2003 Microsoft Excel charting software and considerable experience with the 2007 version. Excel is much more powerful than a counter sorter, but the frustrations are the same. My masters in my quest to earn a black belt in Excel charting were the regular contributors to the *microsoft.public.excel.charting* newsgroup: Rob Bovey, Debra Dalgleish, Shane Devonshire, Bernard Liengme, Tushar Mehta, Jon Peltier, Andy Pope, and John Walkenbach. Over and over again they found solutions to what, for me, were the most unsolvable charting problems. Their replies to my inquiries—and those of thousands of novice and experienced charters—were often simple, direct, and quick, and always courteous.

I am deeply indebted to my colleagues for their encouragement and comments on the convention papers that led to this book and on the initial drafts of the manuscript: Jack Chizmar, Gary King, Nancy Lind, Milo Shields, Howard Wainer, Bill Wilkerson and, much more than a colleague, Patricia Klass. For their proofreading and editing of the manuscript I am indebted for the excellent contributions of three Illinois State graduate students: Jennifer Swanson, Zach Wolfe, and Kara Bavery.

And finally, for their professionalism, encouragement, and assistance, many thanks to Niels Aaboe, Catherine Forrest Getzie, and Asa Johnson at Rowman & Littlefield.

Notes

1. Charles Murray, *Losing Ground: American Social Policy, 1950–1980* (New York: Basic Books, 1984).

2. Jeffrey Sachs, *The End of Poverty: Economic Possibilities for Our Time* (New York: Penguin Press, 2005).

3. The Worldwatch Institute, *The State of the World, 2006* (New York: W. W. Norton, 2006).

4. Bjorn Lomborg, *The Skeptical Environmentalist* (Cambridge: Cambridge University Press, 2001).

5. Kevin Phillips, *The Politics of Rich and Poor: Wealth and the American Electorate in the Reagan Aftermath* (New York: HarperPerrenial, 1991).

6. Paul Krugman, *The Conscience of a Liberal* (New York: W. W. Norton, 2007).

7. Robert D. Putnam, *Bowling Alone* (New York: Simon and Schuster, 2000), 419.

8. Edward Tufte, *The Visual Display of Quantitative Information* (Cheshire, Conn.: Graphics Press, 1993).

9. Howard Wainer, *Visual Revelations: Graphical Tales of Fate and Deception from Napoleon Bonaparte to Ross Perot* (Mahwah, N.J.: Lawrence Erlbaum, 1997).

1

Analyzing Political, Social, and Economic Indicators

Yes, but the numbers I have are very true, and even if some people think I am not black enough for them, the numbers speak for themselves.—Bill Cosby

BILL COSBY IS WRONG: numbers never speak for themselves, but the point he is trying to make is entirely valid.[1] Cosby's declaration is a reply to those who criticized his controversial speech at the 2004 NAACP gala commemorating the fiftieth anniversary of the *Brown v. Board of Education* decision. Cosby was accused of hypocrisy, embracing inauthentic middle-class values, expressing contempt for the plight of the black poor, coddling white audiences, and lending aid to those who really do not care about black America.[2] Had Cosby responded in kind—as many talk show hosts who embraced his remarks did—the media frenzy that ensued might have been more entertaining. Instead, he responded with a book, coauthored with Alvin F. Poussaint, challenging his critics to account for a litany of statistics describing the lives of young black men in America. The statistics he cites, of black male murder, crime, imprisonment, high school dropout, unemployment, life expectancy, and homelessness rates, point to serious problems confronting American society.[3] By themselves, the numbers do not suggest a particular course of action or necessarily support any of the solutions Cosby offers, but by shifting the focus of attention from his own motives to the numerical evidence, Cosby moved the debate in a positive direction.

The Use of Social Indicators

Political, social, and economic indicators serve many functions. They are standardized numerical measurements of the performance of societies' institutions, the evidence that grounds public debate over matters of social policy and public affairs, and the tools of social science research directed to identifying solutions to societies' most pressing problems. Most crucially, social indicators are the standards by which citizens measure the performance of their elected officials and governmental agencies and hold them accountable for their work.

During his 1976 campaign for the presidency, candidate Jimmy Carter focused his campaign on the weak economic record of the Ford administration. Carter added two economic indicators, the inflation and unemployment rates, together to calculate a "misery index," and made much of the fact that the number, shown in figure 1.1, stood near record highs at over 13 percent (although it had been falling steadily during much of Ford's time in office). Four years later, the tables were turned when candidate Ronald Reagan pointed out that Carter's misery index had climbed to over 20 percent. Reagan also made much of the Carter administration's record high 74 billion dollar budget deficit, only to see that number triple in his first years in office.

These and other social indicators inform political debate in the United States and across the globe. Most of the leaders of developing nations, and their political opponents, know exactly where their country ranks on Trans-

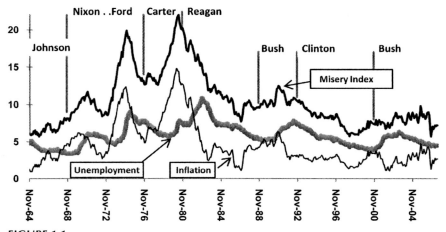

FIGURE 1.1
The Misery Index (inflation + unemployment rate), 1964–2007
Source: The Misery Index (website), http://www.miseryindex.us/.

parency International's measure of political corruption.[4] Few American school principals are unaware of the percentage of their students who score at or below the basic, proficient, and advanced levels on the tests mandated by the No Child Left Behind law. Almost every social policy advocacy group displays a key social indicator statistic prominently on its website: the number of homeless in America, the number of deaths from AIDS, the national poverty rate, the percentage of children who are hungry, the federal debt (updated every second, to the penny), the number of illegal aliens, the number of abortions, or firearm suicides and murder rates.

Those who originally prepared and reported these statistics did so without any assurance as to just how the numbers might be used, but they understood that responsible statistical reporting can have unanticipated beneficial consequences. In 2006, financier Warren Buffet pledged most of his 40 billion dollar wealth to the Bill and Melinda Gates Foundation to support the organization's efforts to address health care needs in developing nations. The Gates foundation was established after Buffet asked Bill Gates to read the disheartening news in the World Bank's *1993 World Development Report,* a detailed statistical summary of economic and health care conditions in the world's poorest nations.[5]

Although collecting and reporting of columns of numbers can be tedious and dispassionate work, the task is not without political ramifications. During the Nixon administration, Ruth Leger Sivard served as chief economist for the U.S. State Department's Arms Control and Disarmament Agency (ACDA) with responsibility for the agency's annual report, *World Military Expenditures,* the most authoritative source of data on military, health, and education spending in countries across the world.[6] In 1972, after the secretary of defense complained to the president that the agency's report undermined congressional support for the defense budget, the agency stopped reporting the education and health data.[7] In response, Sivard resigned her government position, set up her own private nonprofit educational publishing company and, with the help of student volunteers, began publishing her own annual report, *World Military and Social Expenditures,* in competition with the government.[8] More so than the original ACDA report, the new report highlighted the guns and butter trade-offs and the disparities in wealth between the world's rich and poor nations. For her efforts, Sivard received the UNESCO Prize for Peace Education in 1991.

For partisan and nonpartisan policy analysts who seek to identify solutions to the nation's most pressing problems, social indicators provide the answers to the questions they address: Do firearms laws, or the death penalty, reduce murder rates? Would public school students perform better in private schools? Do tax cuts spur economic growth? Do they favor the rich? Do motorcycle helmet and seat belt laws reduce traffic fatalities? Are racial and gender disparities in income and poverty a consequence of societal discrimination? Does national health insurance result in better health care?

It is true, as we will see, that the answer to these questions is seldom clear-cut and the "statistics" are often used to deceive and mislead. But analyses and arguments grounded in a thoughtful analysis of statistical evidence have many advantages over the increasingly common alternative: arguments grounded in ideological presupposition and aspersions of motive. The power of political arguments grounded in statistical evidence was illustrated by a rejoinder Senator Daniel Patrick Moynihan (D-NY) often used in political debates: "You are entitled to your own opinion," he would say, "but you are not entitled to your own facts."[9] Statistical deceptions are often transparent and those who understand how the statistics are calculated, the limitations of the data, and the limitations of the methods of analysis will not be easily fooled. It is a lot easier to show that an interpretation of a statistic is false than it is to disprove allegations that people or groups take particular policy positions because "Liberals hate America" or "Conservatives hate the poor."

Constructing Social Indicators: Count, Divide, and Compare

Analyzing and interpreting social indicators requires a competent understanding of where the data come from, how the data are collected, and how the indicators are constructed. In general, there are three components involved in the use of any social indicator: the counts, the divisors, and the comparisons.[10]

The Counts

The defining element of a social indicator is the statistic's numerator: the counts. Most social indicator counts are based on enumerations derived from either survey questions or agency records. In the case of U.S. infant mortality rate statistics, for example, the "counts" of infant deaths are obtained from tallies of local death certificates (the divisors, from enumerations of birth certificates). To measure unemployment rates, the counts of the unemployed are derived from monthly random sample surveys involving several survey questions concerning the respondents' employment status. (Many people erroneously assume that unemployment rates are based on enumerations of unemployment insurance claims.) Some measures of voter turnout are based on counts of the number of voters who show up at the polls; others, the number of votes cast; still others are based on estimates derived from postelection surveys—counts of respondents who claimed they have voted. Poverty rates may be based on counts of the number of persons living in poor families or counts of the number of poor families. The Federal Bureau of Investigation's crime rate statistics are based on counts of specific crimes reported to local police departments. The Bureau of Justice Statistics calculates a different crime rate statistic using counts of respondents' reports of crimes in household surveys.

Interpreting the social indicators, and avoiding misinterpretations, requires a good understanding of the actual survey questions and definitions and standards used to determine the counts. What seems to be a straightforward statistic is often the product of a quite complex process. To count the number of families living in poverty, for example, the Census Bureau first has to determine the levels of income below which different size families will be considered poor. Then it must determine what constitutes a family's income (food stamps and earned income tax benefits are not counted, welfare and social security payments are). Think that is easy? Now imagine what goes into defining exactly what is and is not a family.

The Divisors

Most social indicators consist of both a numerator (the count) and a denominator (the divisor). For any given social indicator count—such as health care expenditures shown in table 1.1—a variety of social indicators can be constructed using different denominators. Measuring health care expenditures as a percentage of gross domestic product (GDP) is a standard method of adjusting the data for differences in the size of the national economies. National health care expenditures can also be reported per capita, to adjust for the size of the countries' populations; in U.S. dollars, to adjust for differences in currency, weighted by the Organisation for Economic Co-operation and Development (OECD) purchasing power parity (PPP) index, and to adjust for differences in prices.

Common divisors used in the construction of social indicators are population (e.g., murders per 100,000 population), gross domestic product (military expenditures as a percent of GDP), and median family income (university tuition and fees as a percent of median family income). Other indicators use divisors tailored for specific counts. Highway fatality rates are often measured per 100 million vehicle miles traveled, but also per 100,000 licensed drivers, per 100,000 vehicles registered, and per 100,000 population. Abortion *rates* measure the number of abortions per 1,000 women. Abortion *ratios* measure the number of abortions per 1,000 live births.

Careful attention to the divisor is often crucial to statistical analysis. It is possible for the abortion rate to increase at the same time the abortion ratio is in decline. Sparsely populated states usually have very low traffic fatality

TABLE 1.1
Health Expenditure Divisors:
Total Health Expenditures, Selected OECD Nations, 2003

	% of GDP	Per capita US$ PPP*	% Public	Public: % of GDP	% Annual Growth Rate 1998–2003
Ireland	7.3	2,386	75	5.5	11.4
Finland	7.4	2,118	77	5.7	4.1
Austria	7.6	2,280	70	5.3	1.8
Spain	7.7	1,835	71	5.5	2.6
United Kingdom	7.7	2,231	83	6.4	5.7
Hungary	7.8	1,115	70	5.5	6.0
Japan	7.9	2,139	82	6.4	3.0
New Zealand	8.1	1,886	79	6.4	3.4
Italy	8.4	2,258	75	6.3	3.1
Denmark	9.0	2,763	83	7.5	2.8
Sweden	9.2	2,594	85	7.8	5.4
Australia	9.3	2,699	68	6.3	4.1
Portugal	9.6	1,797	70	6.7	3.7
Netherlands	9.8	2,976	62	6.1	4.6
Canada	9.9	3,003	70	6.9	4.2
France	10.1	2,903	76	7.7	3.5
Norway	10.3	3,807	84	8.6	5.3
Iceland	10.5	3,115	84	8.8	5.9
Germany	11.1	2,996	78	8.7	1.8
Switzerland	11.5	3,781	59	6.7	2.8
United States	**15.0**	**5,635**	**44**	**6.7**	**4.6**
Average	9.3	2,682	74	6.7	4.3

*PPP: adjusted for purchasing power parity.
Source: OECD, *Health at a Glance—OECD Indicators 2005*, http://dx.doi.org/10.1787/132836124886

rates measured in terms of the miles traveled, but high fatality rates when population is the divisor. Military expenditures as a percent of GDP may go into decline only because the economy is rapidly growing.

The Comparisons

The purpose of any measurement is to make a comparison. Most analyses of social indicators involve one or a combination of three forms of numerical comparison: cross-sectional comparisons, cross-time comparisons, and comparisons across demographic categories.

The health expenditure data shown in table 1.1 involves cross-sectional comparisons. Cross-sectional comparisons often involve comparing performance measures across nations, states, cities, or institutions, often to make the point

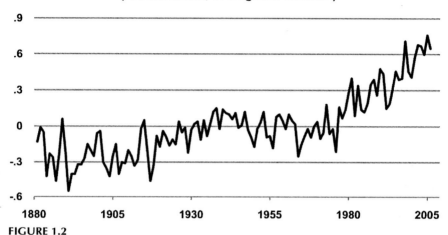

Global Surface Temperature Anomalies
(Annual Mean, in Degrees Celsius)

FIGURE 1.2
Time Series Data
Source: Goddard Institute for Space Studies, "NASA Surface Temperature Analysis (GISTEMP)," http://data
.giss.nasa.gov/gistemp/.

that a particular jurisdiction is doing better or worse than the standards
achieved by others. Thus, as we will see in chapter 5, a national task-force report
on the conditions of American education, *A Nation at Risk*, begins by describing the relatively poor performance of American students on international
mathematics and science tests.[11] Studies of the American death penalty or gun
control laws often begin by citing the statistical evidence that the United States
has the highest murder rate of any developed nation. Studies of American
health policy begin by noting that among developed nations, the United States
has the highest infant mortality rate, relatively low life expectancy, the highest
level of health care expenditure, and the lowest rates of health insurance coverage. Other studies note the relatively high rates of energy consumption, incar-
ceration, child poverty, inequality, and teenage pregnancy in the United States,
conditions ameliorated, perhaps, by our high GDP and low income taxes.

As we saw in the case of the misery index data, time series comparisons of
social indicators are often the crucial evidence employed in arguments about
politics and public policy. In contemporary political debate, trends in social
policy indicators are most often cited to implicitly or explicitly assign blame
to some governmental agency or officials, but on occasion they are employed
solely to issue public warning of impending adversity. Such is the case with the
most portentous time series comparison of our time: the global temperature
data shown in figure 1.2.

Although for a time this evidence of global warming (represented by the hockey stick shape of the post-1940 trend, first described in the work of Michael E. Mann, Raymond S. Bradley, and Malcolm K. Hughes)[12] was hotly contested, few now question the validity of these data. The policy debates have not ended, however, and additional data and comparisons are now the evidence for debate over forecasts of continued temperature increases, explanations of the causes of the global warming, and evaluations of policy changes that might address the problem.

A great deal of social science research is premised on evidence involving comparisons across demographic categories, such as those defined by age, race, nationality, religion, education, and income level. In the chapter that follows, we will see evidence of demographic disparities in social indicators that have profound and puzzling implications for society and politics: The elderly are more likely to vote than the young. The elderly are much less likely to be poor than are children. Women earn less than men. The rich are getting richer and the poor, poorer. Frequent churchgoers are more likely to vote than nonchurchgoers, or, maybe, lie about whether they have voted.

For the United States, the most disturbing social indicator comparisons are often those that involve race. In almost every American field of study where social indicators are used, race and ethnicity are among the most commonly used demographic comparisons.

The U.S. Census Bureau and almost all federal statistical agencies differ from the bureaus and agencies of most other countries in that the United States classifies people by race and not by religion.[13] The racial classification is the subject of considerable controversy and should not be confused with classifications based on nationality, national origin, or ethnicity. In the past, the Census Bureau divided race into four general categories: American Indian or Alaskan Native, Asian or Pacific Islander, black, and white. Often these were reported as just white, black, and other. Ethnicity, most commonly divided into Hispanic and non-Hispanic, is a separate classification, asked as a separate question on the Census forms. Thus one may see the phrase "Hispanics maybe of any race" as a footnote to many U.S. government statistical tables. Alternatively, the data may be cross-classified as white-non-Hispanic, black, Asian, and Hispanic.

This all became more complicated when, beginning with the 2000 Census, the Bureau added the category of "Native Hawaiian or Other Pacific Islander" to the race category and persons were allowed to classify themselves as more than one race. Because of the multiple race combinations, we now see statistics reported for groups defined by categories such as "black-alone" and "black-alone-or-in-combination." The changes allowed for over one hundred possible ethnic and multiple-racial classifications, but it is rare that as many as seven categories (figure 1.3) are used in reports and tabulations.

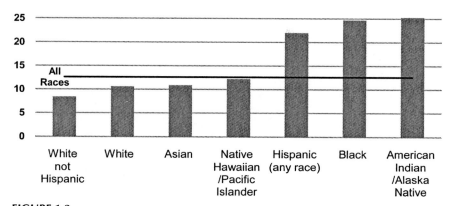

FIGURE 1.3
Census Bureau Racial and Ethnic Categories
Source: U.S. Census Bureau, http://www.census.gov/hhes/www/poverty/poverty05/table5.html.

Combining time series comparisons with cross-sectional or demographic comparisons often provides for a richly detailed analysis. Policy analysts often use the word "skyrocketing" to describe the steadily increasing share of the United States' GDP allocated to health care costs, far outpacing the rate of growth in any other developed nation (figure 1.4). There are many explanations for this phenomenon. The United States is the only industrialized country without universal health care insurance and its fragmented system of public and private insurance lacks any single mechanism for controlling costs.

Time series comparisons are used to evaluate the before and after effects of specific policy changes. The Medicare system, created in 1965, did much to increase demand for medical services but never included any effective cost control measures. The most transformative legislation designed to control health care costs, the 1973 Health Maintenance Organization Act, does not seem to have brought about the anticipated decline in health care costs.

Measurement Validity and Reliability

To evaluate arguments based on social indicators, it is first necessary to determine whether the statistics are trustworthy. Two standards guide the choice and interpretation of a social indicator: measurement validity and measurement reliability. An indicator is valid to the degree that it actually measures the

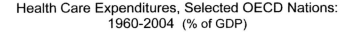

Health Care Expenditures, Selected OECD Nations: 1960-2004 (% of GDP)

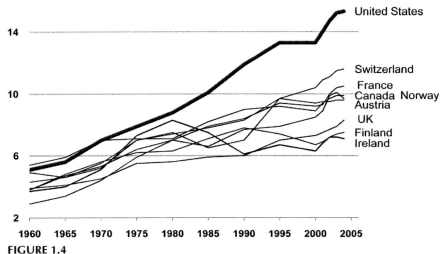

FIGURE 1.4
Cross-Sectional Time Series Data
Source: OECD, http://www.oecd.org/dataoecd/60/28/35529791.xls.

general concept or phenomenon under consideration. An indicator is reliable to the degree that the measurement is consistent.

Measurement Validity

To evaluate the validity of a social indicator, one must consider the context in which it is used and the choices made in determining the indicator's counts and divisors.

Many people question the validity of SAT scores, arguing that the tests do not measure what they are intended to measure, that they measure only a narrow range of intellectual abilities, or that they are culturally or gender biased.[14] Whether an indicator is valid depends on the context and purposes for which it is used. Some insist that the validity of the SAT is confirmed by how well it predicts students' future college performance, but this begs the question of just what it is that is doing the predicting. Because the SAT was at least originally intended to measure some aspect of intellectual ability and not to measure a mastery of the subject matter taught in a particular high school's curricula, scores are probably not a valid indicator of the quality of the instruction in individual high schools or courses. Nevertheless, the often-reported average SAT scores of college and university freshmen classes is probably the best indicator of the selectivity of schools' admission standards.

Often the general concept of interest is ambiguous or, for other reasons, there is no direct measure of the concept at issue. To address this, researchers may combine a variety of different measures of the underlying concept. In his book *Bowling Alone*, Robert Putnam employs several different indicators to measure the concept of social capital, including trends in television viewing, charitable giving, church attendance, volunteerism rates, suicide rates, statewide ballot initiatives, giving the "finger" to other drivers, and (what gives the book its title) participation in league bowling. To measure the level of social capital across the fifty states, Putnam developed a single Social Capital Index, a weighted average of fourteen measures of community life, engagement in public affairs (e.g., voter turnout), volunteerism, and survey responses to questions regarding social trust and sociability.[15]

Similar indexes are used in a wide variety of areas in social science research. In the 1970s, the Overseas Development Council developed a Physical Quality of Life Index (PQLI), a combination of life expectancy, infant mortality, and literacy rates as an alternative to the use of gross national product as a measure of a country's well-being.[16] Later, economist Mahbub ul Haq developed the United Nations' Human Development Index, based on measures per capita of GDP, life expectancy, and education.

Measurement Reliability

If students who took the SAT several different times were likely to get wildly different scores every time (assuming their intellectual ability had remained the same), the test would be unreliable. Unreliability can be caused by errors in data collection, changes in survey procedures, and, occasionally, changes in what people mean by their responses to the same question asked at different periods of times. Even the best data collection efforts are subject to errors that affect data reliability. After several decades of Census undercounts, the Census Bureau's final analysis of the 2000 Census indicated that it had overcounted the nation's population by 1.3 million persons: 5.8 million persons were duplicate counts, 4.5 million not counted at all.[17]

Cross-national data is particularly subject to inconsistent collection and reporting. Although the World Bank, the United Nations, and the OECD, the most authoritative sources for cross-national social and economic indicators, strive to maintain consistent definitions and standards of measurement for the indicators they collect, they rely on national governments and other international organizations for much of their data collection. Especially in developing countries, the isolation of large segments of the population, public suspicion of governmental officials, language barriers, and outright political manipulation of the data can seriously undermine data reliability.

With the exception of data based on agency records, such as birth and death records, data on government budgets, and decennial census indicators based on counts of the whole population, almost all social indicator statistics are obtained from surveys of a relatively small sample of the targeted population. Most public opinion polling data are based on sample sizes ranging from 400 to 1,600 persons. U.S. government social indicators are often based on much larger sample sizes: monthly unemployment rate statistics and annual estimates of poverty rates are based on surveys of 77,000 households.

Because not all of the population is surveyed, estimates derived from samples are not exact and are subject to a "sampling error" that depends for the most part on the sample size. Larger samples have less sampling error. For public opinion polling, sampling error can be estimated using this simple formula:[18]

$$sampling\ error = \frac{1}{\sqrt{N}} * 100$$

Thus, for polls with a sample size (N) of 400, the sampling error is plus or minus 5 percent; for sample sizes of 1,600, it is 2.5 percent. Quadrupling the sample size reduces the error by half. This common estimate of sampling error calculates the error for a 95 percent confidence interval. Thus, if a poll of 400 likely voters finds that 52 percent will vote for the Democratic candidate, we can be 95 percent confident that between 47 percent and 57 percent of the population of likely voters would have indicated that they would vote for the Democrat. How confident you can really be in such a number, however, depends on how confident you can be in the poll's method of determining who the likely voters are. Polling organizations, however, rarely release this information.

Sampling error—the errors in measurement caused by using a small sample to represent the whole population—is just one aspect of measurement reliability, and a highly overrated aspect at that. The estimates of the 95 percent confidence interval are based on a premise that is almost always false: that the persons sampled constitute a random sample of the targeted population. The seeming precision of the sampling error estimate belies all sorts of other sources of unreliability in sampling, particularly those caused by low response rates to the polls. Not everybody is at home when the surveyors appear at the door; many people do not have telephones; people with cell phones (often, college students) cannot be contacted even with the customary random-digit dialing; and many people simply refuse to answer the surveys. For these rea-

TABLE 1.2
Press Reporting of Polling Reliability:
Google News Search "Hits"

Search Terms	Hits
"plus or minus" + poll	5,130
"plus or minus" + survey	3,650
"margin of error of plus or minus"	2,280
"response rate" + poll	44

November 22, 2006.

sons, one should always be wary of the use of sampling error alone as a measure of the reliability of polling results.

Almost every newspaper story reporting public opinion polling data contains a standard sentence indicating the sample size and that the poll has a "margin of error of plus or minus X percent." News stories hardly ever contain any information about the poll's response rate, a fact I confirmed by "Googling" the phrases commonly used in poll news stories (see table 1.2). If election pollsters and their newspaper sponsors were to report response rates: the percentage of those they tried to contact who actually answered the questions, the public would know a lot more about the reliability of their polls than they do from the sampling error statistic.

One commendable poll that always reports information on its response rate is the poll of Elvis fan club presidents conducted by ElvisNew.com. The report of the 2004 poll stated that 47 of the 344 surveys mailed out came back marked "return to sender." On the other hand, this may have been the nonrespondents way of indicating their favorite Elvis song.[19]

The much larger polls used to derive estimates for many U.S. government social indicator estimates have much smaller sampling errors. Census Bureau unemployment and poverty estimates derived from the Current Population Survey report a .2 percent sampling error (using a more liberal 90 percent confidence interval). The larger sample size is necessary to produce reliable estimates for subgroups of the sample. Governmental agencies also have much higher response rates: well over 90 percent for the monthly Current Population Survey. Most polling agencies would be happy with 40 percent response rates.

Reliability and Validity of Crime Statistics

In the 1930s, the Federal Bureau of Investigation began collecting crime statistics, producing a Uniform Crime Report (UCR), a monthly index of violent and property crimes reported to the Bureau by federal, state, and local police agencies. For decades, the UCR data was regarded as the authoritative measure of the nation's crime rate and the FBI worked with state and local agencies to assure that the agencies followed consistent standards in classifying and reporting crimes. Nevertheless, there were serious questions about the reliability of the UCR crime measure. Not all crimes are reported to the police and at least some police agencies lack the technical sophistication or the political incentive to tabulate all the crimes that were reported to them. These factors would combine to make it appear that the least competent and professional police agencies had lower crimes rates. Over time, an increasing willingness of crime victims to report crimes to the police, particularly sexual assault, would also tend to make it appear that crime is increasing when it is not.

Partly to correct these problems, in 1972 the Bureau of Justice Statistics began an annual public survey, the National Crime Victimization Survey (NCVS), of over 77,000 households to measure the incidence of rape, sexual assault, robbery, assault, theft, household burglary, and motor vehicle theft. Although the NCVS survey has some random sampling error, and the samples are too small to produce reliable estimates for all but the nation's largest cities, it is a highly consistent measure of national crime trends and is regarded as more reliable than the FBI data. Nevertheless, there remain problems with the reliability of NCVS crime estimates and an unknown number of crimes still go unreported. One person in each household is asked to report the crimes committed against each member of the household; in cases where the person being interviewed has committed assaults against other family members, the crimes will probably go unrecorded.[20]

The nation's violent crime rates are the most commonly reported NCVS and UCR statistics. Because murder was not included in the survey (murder victims tend not to respond to surveys), the NCVS violent crime estimates includes the UCR murder rate figure (which is assumed to be reliably reported) in its estimate of total violent crime. As we see in figure 1.5, the two measures reveal quite different results. The UCR data indicate that the violent crime rate has increased 25 percent since 1973, while the NCVS estimate has declined by two-thirds.

Generally, researchers conclude that the true crime rate parallels the NCVS trend and that the UCR trend has not declined as dramatically because of better police department record keeping and a greater willingness among the public to report crimes to the police.

Similar questions as to the reliability and validity of social indicators arise in the case of unemployment rate statistics. The Bureau of Labor Statistics provides two different employment statistics, one based on household surveys (similar to the NCVS survey) and another based on a payroll survey of busi-

Violent Crime Rates: FBI Uniform Crime Report and National Crime Victimization Survey, per 1,000 population

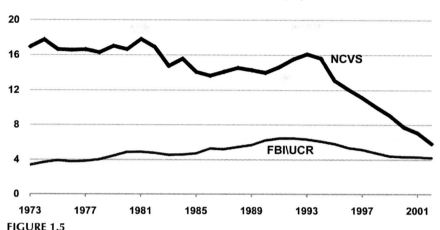

FIGURE 1.5
Two Measures of Violent Crime
Source: Bureau of Justice Statistics, http://www.ojp.usdoj.gov/bjs/glance/cv2.htm.

ness establishments. The household survey is the basis for the most commonly reported unemployment statistic, while the payroll survey provides a general measure of the health of the economy. In recent years (particularly from 2001 to 2003), the two numbers have diverged widely, with the household survey indicating much better economic news coming out of the post-9/11 recession. There are problems with the payroll survey because it is based on surveys from existing business establishments and does not count the self-employed. The household survey, on the other hand, suffers from nonresponse biases (for example, people who are paid cash to avoid taxes) and its reliance on "proxy responses" by household members.[21]

Evaluating Causal Relationships

Jimmy Carter did not point out President Ford's 13 percent misery index statistic just because he wanted Americans to appreciate how miserable they were. He wanted voters to draw the conclusion the President Ford had done something to cause their misery. In effect, he wanted voters to draw a causal connection from an observed relationship.

Observed relationships based on social indicator comparisons across jurisdictions, time, and demographic groups provide direct evidence in support of descriptive conclusions about social phenomena. Comparing poverty rates, for example, the evidence of observed relationships would support the following descriptive conclusions:

- Child poverty rates in the United States are higher than in any other industrialized democracy (figure 6.4, chapter 6).
- The U.S. poverty rates fell during the Clinton administration, then rose under the Bush administration (figure 6.9, chapter 6).
- Poverty rates are higher for African American families than white families (figure 1.3).

The most important, crucial, and problematic uses of social indicator comparisons are when observed relationships are used as evidence to support conclusions about causal relationships. Thus, the same poverty rate relationships that supported these descriptive conclusions might be used to draw these conclusions about causal relationships:

- American child poverty rates are high because the United States lacks the family-oriented social welfare programs common in European nations.
- Clinton administration tax and welfare policies led to a reduction in poverty rates.
- Racial disparities in U.S. poverty rates are a consequence of systemic American racism and discrimination.

Beginning with evidence of a relationship that supports a descriptive conclusion and then drawing a conclusion that implies causation usually requires both additional statistical evidence and a whole lot of reasoning and analysis. Data are just one part of causal arguments; no amount of empirical evidence alone is sufficient to support a claim that any social phenomenon is caused by something else. Ideally, causal claims are grounded in well-reasoned theoretical arguments and are supported by examples and illustrations in addition to the data that define the relationship.

To discount the possibility that an observed relationship is not a causal relationship, one must assess the alternative explanations for the relationship. To be confident that an observed relationship is indeed a causal relationship, it is necessary to rule out the competing reasonable alternative explanations of the relationship.

If we find an observed relationship between two variables, X and Y, we can conclude that X causes Y if it is *not the case* that

- There is no real relationship. This would be the case if the relationship is due to unreliable data measurement. If the observed relationship is within the bounds of sampling error, it is considered not statistically significant. Alternatively, there may be an underlying relationship, but the size of the relationship and the sample size are too small to be confident that it exists.

Other forms of measurement unreliability may also account for the observed relationship. In chapter 4, we will see that voter turnout in the 2004 election, as measured by the American National Election Survey, reached its highest level in forty years. The reasons for the increase, however, are due almost entirely to the survey's declining response rate and other sources of measurement unreliability.

- *Y causes X*. Nations with the highest rates of poverty often have the highest rates of political corruption (see figure 6.2, chapter 6). Does corruption cause poverty, or poverty the corruption? American states with high rates of political corruption tend to have lower rates of voter turnout (see figure 3.26, chapter 3). Does the low turnout cause more corruption or does the corruption lead to fewer people voting?

  One variant on the *Y* causes *X* phenomenon is statistical regression. Governments often implement innovative public policies in response to random negative changes in the underlying social indicator. A state might implement a crackdown on speeding, or pass new drunk driving laws, in response to a sudden increase in highway fatalities and conclude that the program has had the desired effect when the fatality rate returns to normal.[22]

- Something else, related to *X*, causes *Y*. When this occurs, we say that the original relationship was spurious. Are the racial disparities in poverty due to racism or to the high rates of black single parenthood? Did Clinton administration policies, or something else that happened at the same time, produce the decline in poverty rates?

Arguments that erroneously draw causal conclusions from a descriptive relationship most often involve a logical fallacy, specifically a form of the *cum hoc ergo propter hoc* (Latin for "with this, therefore because of this") fallacy.

The possibility that some other variables account for an observed relationship is the reason why we have social scientists. Physical scientists have a convenient method for discounting the possibility that some other factors account for the relationships that they observe: the experiment. More often than not, social scientists who would conduct experiments find themselves under severe constraints. It would be hard to design a controlled experiment to determine whether single parenthood is a cause of poverty or whether the death penalty deters crime.

In the absence of an experimental setting, the most reasonable method for assessing whether a relationship is spurious is to make additional comparisons and examine additional relationships that control for the confounding variables.

Controlling for Spurious Relationships

Often the most important tabulations in a research report are those that control for various factors that might account for, or elaborate, an observed relationship. African Americans are less likely to vote than white Americans, but when one compares voters with equal age, education, and income, the voter turnout rates are very similar (figure 4.5, chapter 4). One school district may have lower math scores than another, but for students of similar family backgrounds it may actually be doing better (figure 5.11, chapter 5).

In table 1.3, we begin with a base relationship indicating that in 2003 women's earnings were only 70 percent of men's. For some, this measure of the disparity in earnings might be sufficient to support causal conclusions about gender discrimination, but others might insist that age, education, and

TABLE 1.3
Controlling for Age and Education:
Mean Earnings, Full-Time, Year-Round Workers,
by Age, Educational Attainment, and Sex: 2003

	Male	*Female*	*Female:* *% of Male*
Total	$53,039	$37,197	70.1
By Age			
18 to 24 years	23,785	20,812	87.5
25 to 34 years	41,993	35,845	85.4
35 to 44 years	56,515	39,234	69.4
45 to 54 years	61,291	40,335	65.8
55 to 64 years	65,765	39,448	60.0
65 years and over	58,398	30,927	53.0
By Level of Education			
Less than 9th Grade	23,972	20,979	87.5
9th to 12th Grade	29,100	21,426	73.6
High School Graduate	38,331	27,956	72.9
Some College, No Degree	46,332	31,655	68.3
Associate Degree	48,683	36,528	75.0
Bachelor's Degree	69,913	47,910	68.5
Master's Degree	85,628	57,635	67.3
Professional Degree	148,331	84,091	56.7
Doctorate Degree	105,648	84,588	80.1

Source: U.S. Census Bureau, Current Population Survey, "Historical Income Tables—People," table P-32, http://www.census.gov/hhes/www/income/histinc/p32.html.

a wide range of other factors should also be considered. As we further examine table 1.3, we see that the relationship is more complex: the earnings gap is lower for younger and less educated men and women.

A full understanding of the relationship between age, education, gender, and earnings would require an even more elaborate breakdown, especially when we consider that the differences in education between men and women vary considerably by age. Although women in the youngest age group earn 88 percent of what men do, women in that age group are actually more likely to have earned college degrees.

Often choosing an appropriate indicator serves to eliminate alternative explanations. In table 1.3, using data for "full-time, year-round workers" eliminates the possibility that the earnings gap is due to women who only work part-time.

Simpson's Paradox

A common manifestation of a spurious relationship is the phenomenon of Simpson's paradox. Simpson's paradox occurs when a relationship that exists for all subgroups of a population disappears when the data are aggregated for the whole population (or the reverse in the case where there is no relationship among the subgroups). Gerald Bracey illustrates the paradox at work in the case of SAT verbal scores.[23] The average verbal score for 2002 was unchanged from the score twenty-one years earlier (table 1.4), yet every subgroup of students taking the test recorded an increase in their scores. Critics of American education who cite the national average scores, Bracey

TABLE 1.4
An Example of Simpson's Paradox:
SAT Verbal Scores, by Race and Ethnicity

	1981	2002	Gain
White	519	527	+8
Puerto Rican	437	455	+18
Mexican	438	446	+8
Black	412	431	+19
Asian	474	501	+27
American Indian	471	479	+8
All Students	504	504	0

Source: Gerald Bracey, "Those Misleading SAT and NAEP Trends." Gerald Bracey (2003), "Those Misleading SAT and NAEP Trends: Simpson's Paradox at Work," Education Disinformation Detection and Reporting Agency, http://www.america-tomorrow.com/bracey/EDDRA/EDDRA30.htm.

argues, unfairly claim that there has been no improvement over the two decades.

How is it possible that all the ethnic groups have done better, but the country as a whole has not improved at all? Look closely at the data in table 1.4 and consider that white students composed 85 percent of the test takers in 1981, but only 65 percent of the test takers in 2002.

Ecological Fallacy

Drawing an erroneous inference about individual behavior from a relationship based on aggregated geographical data can lead to an "ecological fallacy." Sociologist William S. Robinson coined the term in a 1950 article in which he observed that states with the highest rates of foreign-born population also had the highest literacy rates, even though the foreign-born population had lower literacy rates than the native-born population.[24] In figure 1.6, we see that high income states actually have lower rates of homeownership than less wealthy states, but it would be an ecological fallacy to conclude from this that wealthy people are less likely to own homes. As we see in figure 1.7 high income households have, as would be expected, higher rates of homeownership.

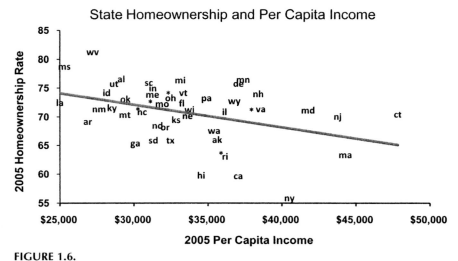

FIGURE 1.6.

Income and Homeownership: Aggregate Data

Source: U.S. Cenus Bureau, Housing Vacancies and Homeownership, 2005, table 13, http://www.census .gov/hhes/www/housing/hvs/annual05/ann05t13.html.

Homeownership Rates by Income Quartile

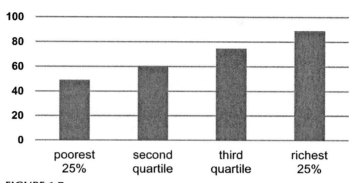

FIGURE 1.7
Income and Homeownership: Household Data
Source: Economic Policy Institute, The State of Working America, 2006–2007, http://www
.stateofworkingamerica.org/.

Cherry Picking

Cherry picking, the selective culling of evidence to support a claim is a common problem in political debate and social science research. With time series analysis, cherry picking can involve the arbitrary selection of beginning and ending time points. Imagine that you are a candidate of either the incumbent or the opposition party at the time of any of the elections shown in the misery index chart in figure 1.1. Can you find a period of time before the election when the misery index went up? Can you find a time period when it went down?

Many of the claims that tax cuts actually result in increasing government revenues, based on an economic theory known as the Laffer curve, often cite evidence of improving economic performance and rising revenues over a period of time following the tax cuts.

In 1981, Congress and the Reagan administration enacted the biggest tax cuts in U.S. history, reducing the top marginal rate from 70 percent in 1981 to 50 percent in 1982.[25] Proponents of what was called Reaganomics often credit the economic growth of the 1980s and the doubling of federal government revenues in the 1980s. Heritage Foundation economist Daniel Mitchell (2003) argues the point: "Once the economy received an unambiguous tax cut in January 1983, income tax revenues climbed dramatically, increasing by more than 54 percent by 1989 (28 percent after adjusting for inflation)." [26]

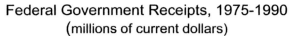

Federal Government Receipts, 1975-1990
(millions of current dollars)

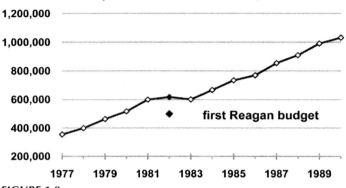

FIGURE 1.8
Cherry Picking Budget Data
Source: Budget of the United States: Historical Tables, table 1.1, http://www
.gpoaccess.gov/usbudget/fy07/hist.html.

Note how Mitchell does provide a reason for selecting 1983 as his base year (even though the tax cut was in effect for the last nine months of fiscal year 1982), but it seems more than convenient that he does not explain the startling decline in revenues in 1983 (figure 1.8). Had he chosen 1981 as the base year—the year before the tax cuts went into effect—the revenue increases would not be as dramatic. Mitchell also neglects to mention the tax increases that Reagan signed in 1982 and 1984, necessitated, many thought at the time, by the huge deficits created in 1982 and 1983.

Mitchell also fails to note the economic growth and increased revenue that followed the 1993 Clinton tax increases and that led to the first budget surplus in thirty years. Mitchell did know about Clinton's tax increase: in 1993, he wrote that the Clinton tax increase was the "biggest tax increase in American history" and predicted that it would reduce economic growth and lead to even bigger budget deficits.[27] The budget surpluses (reducing the national debt) following the Clinton tax increase lasted until George W. Bush cut taxes in 2001. The effect of the tax cuts and increases on the national debt is shown in figure 1.9.

The selective cherry picking of evidence is rarely done intentionally. Political commentators, politicians, and policy analysts naturally seek out evidence that confirms their own previously held beliefs and are generally suspicious about evidence that does not. Note that in presenting counterevidence to Mitchell's arguments, I have also cherry picked my own evidence.

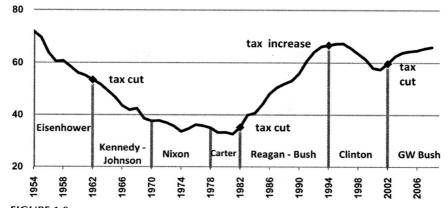

FIGURE 1.9
National Debt (% of GDP), 1954–2008
Source: Budget of the United States, 2008, Historical Tables, table 7.1.

The Rate of Change Fallacy

A general theme of Andrew Hacker's 1995 book *Two Nations*, a widely respected analysis of race in American society, is that racism is the underlining cause of the worsening social and economic disparities affecting black America.[28] The book counters the claims of conservatives (such as in Charles Murray's 1980 book, *Losing Ground*) that liberal social policies and the rise in black single-parent families are to blame for the conditions in black America. Throughout the book, Hacker includes a number of tables, similar to table 1.5-A, containing measures of black and white social conditions and, as a measure of the disparity between the two races, a "Black Multiple," in this case measuring the ratio of black to white out-of-wedlock birth rates.

From these data, Hacker concludes that "even though the number of births to unwed black women has ascended to an all-time high, white births outside of marriage have been climbing at an even faster rate."[29] He does not say it, but the implication is that the rise in single-parent families should not be seen as a black problem, but as a general societal phenomenon.

The problem with Hacker's conclusion is that it depends on what you mean by "climbing at a faster rate." It is true that the 1992 white unwed birth rate is more than ten times higher than the 1950 rate, while the 1992 black rate is only three times higher. On the other hand, the white rate is a net change of only 16 percentage points, while the black rate has a net increase of almost 50 percentage points. If the black out-of-wedlock birth rate had risen to 100 percent, Hacker's analysis would still conclude that the white rate was climbing faster.

TABLE 1.5
Comparing Changes in Rates

Year	Black*	White	Black Multiple
A. Out-of-Wedlock Birth Rate, by Race: 1950–1992			
(percent of all births)			
1950	16.8	1.7	9.9
1960	21.6	2.3	9.4
1970	37.6	5.7	6.6
1980	56.4	9.3	6.1
1992	68.3	18.5	3.7
B. In-Wedlock Birth Rate, by Race: 1950–1992			
(percent of all births)			
1950	83.2	98.3	0.8
1960	78.4	97.7	0.8
1970	62.4	94.3	0.7
1980	43.6	90.7	0.5
1992	31.7	81.5	0.4

*Excludes Hispanic births after 1960.
Source: Hacker, Two Nations, 84.

Hacker has committed a rate-of-change fallacy: comparing rates of change (usually rates of changes in rates) in two numbers that start out at different levels. Another way of looking at this data, shown in table 1.5-B, is to consider the in-wedlock birth rate instead of the out-of-wedlock birth rate. Had Hacker used these data, the reciprocal of his own numbers, he would have to draw the opposite conclusion: that the black in-wedlock birth rate is falling much faster than the white in-wedlock rate. Hacker's conclusion is not wrong so much as it is incomplete and misleading.

Examining a Relationship: New York City Crime Rates

Throughout his 2008 campaign, Republican presidential candidate Rudy Giuliani has highlighted his accomplishments as mayor of New York City, particularly his record in reducing the city's crime rate. One news account, in the *Economist,* summarizes the record: "Crime halved under Mr. Giuliani and murders fell by two-thirds, transforming New York from one of the most dangerous cities in America to one of the safest."[30]

These reductions in crime are significant not only in terms of the support they lend to the Giuliani campaign, but also because they are often cited as evidence of the success of a dramatic and controversial strategy of policing large cities. Soon after Giuliani became mayor in January 1994, he appointed

TABLE 1.6
Crime Rates in the Nation's Largest-City Police Departments, 1993 and 2004

	1993	2004	Net Change	% Change
*Violent Crime Rates**				
Chicago	2,717	1,218	−1,500	−55
Los Angeles	2,374	686	−1,688	−71
New York City	2,090	687	−1,402	−67
Metro-Dade	1,881	823	−1,058	−56
Dallas	1,743	1,316	−428	−25
Los Angeles County	1,695	1,107	−588	−35
Houston	1,454	1,146	−307	−21
Philadelphia	1,255	1,408	153	+12
San Diego	1,160	529	−631	−54
Phoenix	1,146	662	−484	−42
Las Vegas Metro	1,015	789	−226	−22
San Antonio	682	635	−47	−7
*Murder Rates**				
Los Angeles	30.5	16.2	−14	−47
Dallas	30.4	20.2	−10	−34
Chicago	30.3	15.5	−15	−49
Philadelphia	28.1	22.2	−6	−21
New York City	26.5	7.0	−20	−74
Houston	25.9	13.3	−13	−49
Los Angeles County	24.2	13.4	−11	−45
San Antonio	22.3	7.6	−15	−66
Metro-Dade	16.6	7.9	−9	−52
Phoenix	15.2	14.1	−1	−7
Las Vegas Metro	12.7	10.6	−2	−17
San Diego	11.5	4.8	−7	−58

*Rates per 100,000 population.
Source: Bureau of Justice Statistics, Data Online, (FBI UCR) http://bjsdata.ojp.usdoj.gov/dataonline/Search/
    Crime/Local/LocalCrimeLarge.cfm.

William J. Bratton as police commissioner. Bratton initiated a new policing
strategy involving the use of CompStat (a new computerized system for track-
ing and responding to changes in neighborhood crime), a crackdown on less
serious crimes (such as graffiti and subway turnstile jumping), the use of "stop
and frisk" searches for illegal handguns (this, not highlighted in the candidate's Republican presidential campaign), restrictions on the homeless, and a
variety of other aggressive policing measures that drove civil libertarians to
outrage.

Few contest that there were substantial reductions in crime over the course
of the Giuliani administration, and the FBI Uniform Crime Report data (table

1.6) indicates that the *Economist*, if anything, understates Giuliani's record. Both violent crime and murder rates fell by over two-thirds in New York City between 1993 (the year before Giuliani became mayor) and 2004 (his last year in office). By these data, New York City was indeed one of the most dangerous large cities in 1993, and second only to San Diego, one of the safest in 2004. The City of Los Angeles did record a higher percentage drop in violent crime rates over this time,[31] but its murder rate remained relatively high.

Nevertheless, Giuliani's critics dispute the claim that the mayor and his policies were responsible for the reductions. Giuliani biographer, Wayne Barrett, argues that the decline in the crime rates began under the previous mayor, David Dinkins, and the reasons for the decline had more to do with general national economic prosperity of the 1990s that led crime rates to fall in other cites at the same time. Most significant, Barrett insists that the Giuliani administration manipulated the crime statistics: "Rudy Giuliani is not a management expert, he is a statistical expert. He has jimmied every number we live by."[32] Most of the crime reduction, he adds, was for nonviolent crimes such as larcenies under fifty dollars (15 percent of the reduction) and auto and auto-parts theft (42 percent of the reduction).

Barrett is correct in noting that some crime reduction did take place in the later years of the Dinkins administration: the city's murder rate fell during his last three years in office, after years of steady increases. It would be unfair not to give Dinkins some credit for the decline in the year after he left office (figure 1.10), or Giuliani for the murder rate drop, from 7.0 to 6.6, the year after he left office.[33]

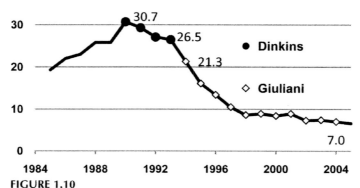

FIGURE 1.10
New York City Murder Rate: Dinkins and Giuliani Administrations
(per 100,000 population)
Source: Bureau of Justice Statistics, Data Online (FBI UCR).

Although the total violent crime rate is the more comprehensive measure of how safe these cities are, the murder rate is a more reliable measure. Police departments have considerable discretion in classifying other violent crimes, and incidents of rape and aggravated assault may not be consistently recorded either over time or across police departments. Giuliani's critics argue that much of the drop in the city's violent crime rate was an artifact of the Comp-Stat system that made neighborhood police commanders acutely aware of their districts' crime rates and provided them an incentive to underreport crime.[34] Presumably, most murders are reported to the police and recorded as such, but even here, there is room for inconsistencies. In 1999, for example, the New York City medical examiner recorded nineteen homicides that were not recorded by the New York Police Department (NYPD). Nevertheless, the discrepancy was less than in 1993 when the NYPD did not report fifty-five of the medical examiner's homicides.[35]

To assess whether the violent crime rate drop was due to underreporting, we have some data for New York City from the National Crime Victimization Survey. The NCVS estimate shown in figure 1.11, constructed by two Bureau of Justice Statistics researchers, Patrick Langan and Matthew Durose, combines the NCVS measures of violent crime victimization and the New York medical examiner murder rate data.[36] The data clearly do not support several of Barrett's claims. The NCVS measures shows violent crime holding pretty steady even through the first year of Giuliani's administration and then falling faster than the crimes reported to the NYPD: the NCVS measures fall by 60

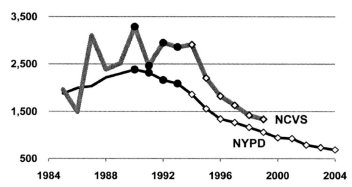

FIGURE 1.11
New York City Violent Crime Rates: NYPD and NCVS Estimates (per 100,000 population)
Sources: NCVS: Langdon and Duross, "The Remarkable Drop in Crime in New York City"; NYPD: Bureau of Justice Statistics, Data Online (FBI UCR).

percent from 1993 to 1999, the NYPD measures only 50 percent. In a more detailed analysis of the data, Langan and Durose find that a higher percentage of crimes were reported to the NYPD after 1993.[37]

Barrett is also correct that most of the crime reduction was for nonviolent crimes. Based on the FBI data, nonviolent crimes fell from 447,000 in 1993 to 187,000 in 2002; violent crimes fell from 154,000 to 64,000. But Barrett's point is nothing but political spin: both numbers fell by an identical 42 percent.

That leaves Barrett's claim that the drop in crime that was not due to statistical manipulation was actually a result of the city's economic prosperity. Most researchers acknowledge that the overall drop in the nation's crime rate in the 1990s was due in large part to the economic growth of the time (following the Clinton tax increases in 1993), and the unusually good economic prosperity New York City enjoyed in the 1990s may account for its success in reducing crime. Separating out the impact of the economy from the impact of Giuliani administration policies would be beside the point, as Giuliani also takes credit for the city's economic prosperity during his administration. When we consider the relationship between New York City's economy and crime rates, it is not clear what causes what; if anything, the economic changes follow the crime rates (figure 1.12).

It may be true that New York City's crime rates would not have fallen as far as they did had it not been for the city's economic performance, but it is also reasonable that the economy would not have done as well as it did had it not been for the drop in the crime rate.

Other, largely nonquantifiable, factors peculiar to the times and the city may have been at work. Among the more intriguing explanations is that declines in children's exposure to lead, beginning in the 1970s, accounted for the

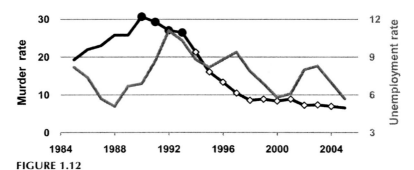

FIGURE 1.12
New York City Murder and Unemployment Rates
Source: New York State Department of Labor, http://www.labor.state.ny.us/workforceindustrydata/.

national reductions in crime in the 1990s. Economist Rick Nevin's research, for example, identifies a strong link between children's exposure to lead and crime rate trends across nine nations.[38] Nevin conjectures that New York City's crime rate may have fallen faster because the city made a serious effort to reduce lead exposure in the 1970s. Also, the high rates of crime and murder in the late 1980s and early 1990s were probably a consequence of the crack cocaine epidemic and New York City's crime rates may have had something to do with the stabilization of the gang-and-cocaine economy in the 1990s.

In cities across America in the 1990s, mayors touted their success in fighting crime in their reelection campaigns. For most, it was dumb luck; they just happened to be in office at the right time. The evidence presented here offers no final proof that the mayor's policies reduced crime. Maybe he was lucky. During Giuliani's eleven years as mayor, the New York Yankees reached the World Series six times and won the series four times, after a fifteen-year drought. Although no other team (for example, in Boston or Chicago) has ever come close to this record, we do not credit the mayor for the success for obvious reasons: he didn't do anything that would have conceivably have had any effect on the team's performance. Nevertheless, Giuliani's record as a crime fighter does withstand considerable scrutiny. He did implement what even his critics must concede were far-reaching changes in policing strategy. The city's crime rates fell more dramatically than in other cities. For the most part, the alternative explanations for the drop in crime do not withstand the scrutiny.

Notes

1. Bill Cosby and Alvin F. Poussaint, *Come On People* (Nashville, Tenn.: Thomas Nelson, 2007), xv.

2. Michael Eric Dyson, *Is Bill Cosby Right? Or Has the Black Middle Class Lost Its Mind?* (New York: Basic Books, 2005).

3. Cosby and Poussaint, *Come On People*, 8–9.

4. The United States was ranked as the twentieth least-corrupt nation in 2006. Transparency International, "2006 Corruption Perceptions Index," November 2006, at www.transparency.org.

5. World Bank, *World Development Report 1993: Investing in Health, volume 1* (New York: Oxford University Press, 1993).

6. United States Arms Control and Disarmament Agency, *World Military Expenditures* (Washington, D.C.: Government Printing Office, 1971).

7. Ruth Leger Sivard, "Speech by Ms. Ruth Leger Sivard, Laureate of the UNESCO Prize 1991 for Peace Education," (Paris: UNESCO, 1992) at unesdoc.unesco.org/images/0012/001227/122733eo.pdf. The 1974 ACDA report says that the data were omitted "partly because of the paucity of data, but also because the omission of private health and education expenditures led to distorted comparisons between free

market and centrally planned economies." See: United States Arms Control and Disarmament Agency, *World Military Expenditures and Arms Trade* (Washington, D.C.: Government Printing Office, 1974), iii.

8. Ruth Leger Sivard, *World Military and Social Expenditures 1974* (Washington, D.C.: World Priorities, Inc., 1974). Thanks to Jim Sivard (jimsivard@verizon.net) for information about his mother.

9. Daniel Patrick Moynihan, quoted in Timothy J. Penny, "Facts Are Facts," *National Review*, September 4, 2003.

10. "Count, Divide, and Compare" is formulation developed by epidemiologists at the Centers for Disease Control (CDC).

11. The National Commission on Excellence in Education, "A Nation at Risk: The Imperative for Educational Reform," April 1983, at www.ed.gov/pubs/NatAtRisk.

12. Michael E. Mann, Raymond S. Bradley, and Malcolm K. Hughes, "Global-Scale Temperature Patterns and Climate Forcing Over the Past Six Centuries," *Nature*, 392: 779–87. Mann, Bradley, and Hughes's original charts were based on reconstruction of temperatures over six hundred years; the data in figure 1.2 are regarded as more reliable data based on meteorological station records.

13. Hate crime statistics are the only exception to this rule; religious hate crimes are classified as anti-Jewish, Catholic, Protestant, Islamic, other, and atheist.

14. See The National Center for Fair and Open Testing, "FairTest" at www.fairtest .org; Nicholas Lemann, *The Big Test: The Secret History of the American Meritocracy* (New York: Farrar, Straus and Giroux, 1999).

15. Robert D. Putnam, *Bowling Alone: The Collapse and Revival of American Community* (New York: Simon and Schuster, 2000).

16. Morris David Morris, *Measuring the Conditions of the World's Poor: The Physical Quality of Life Index* (New York: Pergamon Press, 1979).

17. U.S. Census Bureau Public Information Office, "Statement of Census Bureau Director C. Louis Kincannon on Accuracy and Coverage Evaluation Revision II," U.S. Department of Commerce News, March 12, 2003 (CB03-CS.02) at www.census.gov/Press-Release/www/releases/archives/directors_corner/000813.html.

18. The basic equation for sampling error was "discovered" by Abraham De Moivre, *Miscellanea Analytica* (London: Tonson and Watts, 1730). A more complicated formula provides more precise estimates and should be used when the size of the population, or the sample percentage, is relatively small.

19. Elvis Central, "Report: 6th Annual Independent Survey of Elvis Websites," February 6, 2005, at www.elvisnews.com/Presentation/Functional/Page/articles .aspx=719.

20. Michael R. Rand and Callie M. Rennison, "True Crime Stories? Accounting for Differences in Our National Crime Indicators," *Chance Magazine* 15, no. 1 (Winter 2002): 47–51.

21. Tao Wu, "Two Measures of Employment: How Different Are They?" *Federal Reserve Bank of San Francisco Economic Letter*, Number 2004-23, August 27, 2004, 1–3.

22. Donald T. Campbell and H. Laurence Ross, "The Connecticut Crackdown on Speeding: Time Series Data in Quasi-Experimental Analysis," in *The Quantitative Analysis of Social Problems*, ed. Edward R. Tufte (Reading, Mass.: Addison-Wesley, 1970).

23. Gerald Bracey, "Those Misleading SAT and NAEP Trends: Simpson's Paradox at Work," Education Disinformation Detection and Reporting Agency, posted January 8, 2003, at www.america-tomorrow.com/bracey/EDDRA/EDDRA30.htm.

24. William S. Robinson, "Ecological Correlations and the Behavior of Individuals," *American Sociological Review* 15 (June 1950): 351–57.

25. Tax Foundation, "U.S. Federal Individual Income Tax Rates History, 1913–2007," February 27, 2007, at www.taxfoundation.org/taxdata/show/151.html.

26. Daniel J. Mitchell, "The Historical Lessons of Lower Tax Rates," The Heritage Foundation, August 13, 2003, at www.heritage.org/Research/Taxes/wm327.cfm.

27. Daniel J. Mitchell, "Clinton's Budget: Higher Taxes and More Spending," The Heritage Foundation (Backgrounder #928), February 18, 1993, at www.heritage.org/Research/Budget/BG928.cfm.

28. Andrew Hacker, *Two Nations: Black and White, Separate, Hostile, Unequal* (New York: Balantine Books, 1995).

29. Hacker, *Two Nations*, 86.

30. "From America's Mayor to America's President?" *The Economist*, May 3, 2007, at www.economist.com/world/na/displaystory.cfm?story_id=9119759.

31. William Bratton became Los Angeles city police commissioner in 2002. He left New York City in 1996, allegedly after a dispute with the mayor over who deserved more credit for the city's falling crime rate. See William J. Bratton (with Peter Knobler), *The Turnaround: How America's Top Cop Reversed the Crime Epidemic* (New York: Basic Books, 1998).

32. Wayne Barrett, "Giuliani's Legacy: Taking Credit for Things He Didn't Do," *Gotham Gazette: New York City News and Policy,* June 25, 2001, at www.gothamgazette.com/commentary/91.barrett.shtml.

33. None of the New York City 2001 homicide figures include the 2,823 persons killed at the World Trade Center on September 11.

34. John Eck and Edward Maguire, "Have Changes in Policing Reduced Violent Crime? An Assessment of the Evidence," in *The Crime Drop in America,* Alfred Blumstein and Joel Wallman, eds. (Cambridge: Cambridge University Press, 2000), 207–65.

35. Patrick A. Langan and Matthew R. Durose, "The Remarkable Drop in Crime in New York City" (paper presented at the International Conference on Crime, Rome, Italy, December 2003) samoa.istat.it/Eventi/sicurezza/relazioni/Langan_rel.pdf.

36. Langan and Durose, "The Remarkable Drop," table 1.

37. Langan and Durose, "The Remarkable Drop," 21.

38. Rick Nevin, "Understanding International Crime Trends: The Legacy of Preschool Lead Exposure," *Environmental Research* 104, no. 3 (July 2007): 315–36.

2

Constructing Good Tables

Getting information from a table is like extracting sunbeams from a cucumber.—Arthur Briggs Farquhar and Harry Farquhar[1]

RESEARCH REPORTS AND ANALYSES based on numerical information should accommodate two different audiences: those who read the text but ignore the data presented in tables and charts, and those who skim the text and grasp the main ideas from the data presentation. To serve the latter audience, tables (and charts discussed in the next chapter) should be self-explanatory, conveying the critical ideas contained in the data without relying on the text to explain what the numbers mean. The text should accommodate readers who skim past the numbers, providing a general summary of the most important ideas illustrated by the data—without repeating many of the numbers contained in the tables. When done well, tables will complement the text and permit careful readers to critically evaluate the evidence for the conclusions presented in the text.

There are two types of tables. Just about all of the numerical data included in this book was originally found in "look up" tables, databases, or spreadsheets compiled by government statistical agencies or nongovernmental organizations. The general and limited purpose of these tabulations is to present all the numerical information available that might be relevant to a wide variety of data users. For the most part, the tables' text draws no conclusions about the data and serves only to describe how the data were obtained and to define what the numbers mean. The tables contained in analytical writing, however, serve a different purpose: the presentation of numerical evidence relevant to support specific conclusions contained in the text. To serve this purpose much care must be given to the selection of the data and to the design of the table.

Assuming one has meaningful data that will support the conclusions made in the text, two general principles guide the construction of a table, and any form of data presentation. The data should be unambiguous. The presentation should convey the most important ideas about the data efficiently.

Presenting Unambiguous Data

Whether the information presented in a table is unambiguous depends largely on the descriptive text contained in the titles, headings, and notes. The table titles, column and row headings and subheadings, and footnotes should convey the general purpose of the table, explain coding, scaling, and definition of the variables, and define relevant terms or abbreviations.

The essential idea of a table is to facilitate numerical comparisons by organizing data into rows and columns. In the most common form of a table, the numbers are defined by the table title, column headings, row labels, and notes. Thus in table 2.1, the title indicates that all the numbers in the table are measures of the child poverty rate, which varies across and down the groups specified by the column and row headings. A spanning ("Head of household") column heading defines similar columns. Because of the complicated categories of race and ethnicity used by the U.S. Census, annotations are used to fully define the row label categories.

The titles, headings, and footnotes should precisely define what each number in the table represents. When reporting rates or ratios, both the numerator and denominator should be clearly defined. Pay particular attention to

TABLE 2.1
Components of a Table:
Poverty Rate of Children by Family Status, Race, and Ethnicity, 2005

	Head of Household			
	Married Couple	Single Male	Single Female	All Children
White*	8.0	17.5	38.7	10.0
Asian**	8.3	11.5	24.6	10.3
Black**	11.9	31.0	49.4	33.5
Hispanic	20.1	23.6	50.1	28.3
All races	8.5	19.9	42.6	17.6

*White alone, not Hispanic.
**Race alone or in combination with other races (Hispanics of any race).
Source: U.S. Census, Current Population Survey. 2006 Annual Social and Economic Supplement, table POV01.

whether the raw count numbers are reported in hundreds, thousands, or millions and whether monetary data are in current or constant (inflation adjusted) dollars. The amount of detail given to defining the data depends on the audience. In a paper written for economists, it would not be necessary to define terms like GDP (gross domestic product), unemployment rate (the percentage of the labor force seeking work), or PPP (purchasing power parity); for other audiences more detail may need to be provided.

Table Titles

A complete table (or chart) title fully defines the three components of the social indicator in the table: the count, the divisor, and the comparisons, as in the following examples:

Public and Private Health Care Expenditures: OECD nations (% of GDP)

U.S. Public Health Care Expenditures Per Capita, 1975–2004 (constant 1999 dollars)

Murder Rates in Wealthy Nations, 1999 (homicides per 100,000 population)

State Voter Turnout Rates: Presidential Elections, 1992–2004 (votes cast/ voting age population)

In books, lengthy reports, and theses that contain an index of tables and figures, the titles should include more detail and often include information repeated in the row and column headings. In less formal writing, table titles sometimes state an explicit conclusion more forcefully. Thus, table 2.1 might be titled "Poverty Is Mostly a Function of Family Status, Not Race," with the actual definition of the variables reserved for subtitles and footnotes.

Labeling the Rows and Columns

Column headings and row labels should be as brief and succinct as possible while still fully describing the data. Spanning headings and row spanning row labels ("Head of Household" in table 2.1) are used to eliminate redundant text. Totals and summative measures are best placed on the right-hand columns and either in the top or bottom rows.

Sources

Fully specifying the sources of the data in the table lends authenticity to the numbers presented, expresses a willingness to allow readers to fact-check the data, and for readers familiar with different sources of similar data, aids in defining the data. Although nonacademic writing often contains sketchy and vague citations of data sources (such as "U.S. Census Bureau," or "World Bank"), such practices often indicate sloppy research and should be avoided. A fundamental principle of social science research is that the empirical findings should be replicable.[2] To this end, citations and data definitions should be sufficient to direct readers who would seek to confirm the accuracy of the data to the exact source of the data.

Describing Percentages and Ratios

Percentages can usually be calculated in at least two different ways and are often a source of confusion. Consider the difference between the two tables in table 2.2. In table A, we see that 14 percent of poor families are headed by a householder less than 24 years of age; in table B, 31 percent of families headed by a householder under 24 years old are poor. Although the two table titles clearly define the difference, showing the 100 percent total in table A and the "all families" rate in table B helps convey the correct interpretation more quickly to the reader.

It is not uncommon for writers to use distribution percentages to support conclusions that a particular group is over- or underrepresented on a given measure, even though it often requires a comparison with the groups' population distribution, as in table A. To make the point with table A, one would say that "the elderly represent 10 percent of the nation's poor even though they make up 34 percent of the population." In general, this is an awkward and

TABLE 2.2
Percentage Distributions versus Rates

A: Distribution of Poverty Families, by Age of Householder, 1999			B: Poverty Rate of Families, by Age of Householder, 1999	
Age of Householder	*% of Poor Families*	*% of All Families*	*Age of Householder*	*Poverty Rate*
18 to 24	14%	5%	18 to 24	31%
25 to 34	29	15	25 to 34	16
35 to 44	27	19	35 to 44	10
45 to 54	12	17	45 to 54	6
55 to 64	9	11	55 to 64	6
65 and over	10	34	65 and over	6
Total	*100*	*100*	*All families*	*9*

Source: U.S. Statistical Abstract 2001, CD-Rom, table 686.

TABLE 2.3
Ambiguous Data:
Change in Teenage Birth Rates:
1987–1998

White	6.7%
Black	−4.9
Asian	−1.8
Hispanic	3.7

Source: U.S. Statistical Abstract, 2000,
    table 85.

clumsy way of making this statistical point; using the rate data, as in table B, makes the point much more succinctly.

Change in Percentages

Calculating changes in percentages, rates, and ratios is also a source of confusion both in tabular display and in textual summaries of data. Table 2.3 is an example of poorly defined percentage change data.

Consider the ambiguity of these data by trying to answer the following questions:

- Does the teenage birth rate measure the percentage of all babies who were born to teenage mothers or the percentage of teenage mothers who gave birth?
- What does the change actually measure?

Some readers might interpret the 3.7 percent increase in Hispanic poverty as the result if the rate went from 20 percent to 23.7 percent. Others would view an increase from 20 percent to 27.4 percent as a 3.7 percent increase.

In table 2.4, the change in the married-couple family poverty rate, from 8.3 percent in 1994 to 7 percent in 2003 can be expressed in several different ways:

- The 2003 the poverty rate for all families was 7 percent, 1.3 percentage points lower than the 1994 rate.
- The poverty rate of American families fell 16 percent from 1994 to 2003.
- The 1994 poverty rate is 19 percent higher than the 2003 rate.
- The 2003 poverty rate for families was 84 percent of its 1994 level.

In general, the use of "net change" or "net percentage point change" is the least susceptible to misinterpretation. Calculating the percentage change with

TABLE 2.4
Net Change and Percentage Change:
Poverty Rates of Families with Children, by Family Status, Race, and
Ethnicity, 1994 and 2003

	1994	*2003*	*Net Change*	*% Change*
All Families:	17.4	14.8	−2.6	−16
White*	10.6	8.9	−1.7	−16
Black**	35.9	28.6	−7.3	−20
Hispanic	34.2	25.2	−9.0	−26
Married Couple Families:	8.3	7.0	−1.3	−16
White*	7.5	6.6	−0.9	−12
Black**	11.4	9.1	−2.3	−20
Hispanic	23.9	18.4	−5.5	−23
Single, Female Householder:	44.0	35.5	−8.5	−19
White*	33.5	28.1	−5.4	−16
Black**	53.9	42.7	−11.2	−21
Hispanic	59.2	43.0	−16.2	−27

*White (alone), not Hispanic.
**Black alone or in combination.
Source: U.S. Census Bureau, Historical Poverty Tables, table 4.

the later year as the divisor (as in the third option: "was 19 percent higher") causes unnecessary confusion.

Presenting Data Efficiently

An efficient tabular display will allow a reader to quickly discern the purpose and import of the data and to draw a variety of interesting conclusions from a large amount of information. The measure of a table's efficiency is the number of meaningful comparisons that can readily be drawn from the data presentation. How quickly a reader can digest the information presented, discern the critical relationships among the data, and draw meaningful conclusions depends on how well the table is formatted.

Efficiency is often a matter of balance: more data allows for more comparisons, but too much data can obscure meaningful comparison. A properly formatted table, allows the reader to quickly draw the correct conclusion.

Defining Rows and Columns

As a rule, similar data ought to be presented down the columns of the table. Mixing data of different types in the same column is disorienting. Compare table 2.5 to the same data in table 2.9.

TABLE 2.5
Poor Placement of Cases and Variables in Rows and Columns:
Income, Poverty, and Education, by Race and Hispanic Origin: 1998

	White	Asian*	Hispanic**	Black
Median Family Income	49,023	52,826	29,608	29,404
Poverty Rate	10.1	12.5	25.6	26.1
% High School Graduates	84.3	84.7	56.1	77.0

*Asian and Pacific Islander.
**Hispanics may be of any race.
Source: Statistical Abstract, 2000, tables 250, 737, 755.

Sorting

The "look up" tables of most reference sources generally list data for geographic units (countries, states, or cities) alphabetically. If you are using a table to make a point, the reader will discern the point more quickly if the data are sorted on a meaningful variable. The alphabet is almost never the most meaningful variable. Although Cubs fans might find it inspiring, consider why baseball standings are not presented as they are in table 2.6.

A properly sorted table will reveal things about the data that otherwise would remain hidden. Consider, for example, the advantage of table 2.7-B over the alphabetical sorting in table 2.7-A. See how much more quickly you can indentify the countries where students watch the most and the least TV, the high-to-low variation in the data, and which country (Italy) is the median.

Whether the data are sorted in ascending or descending magnitude is often immaterial, but following the baseball convention, it is often better if the cases that score the "best" on a variable are listed at the top. In the case of tables that present two years of data in adjacent columns, such as table 1.6 in chapter one, it is best to sort the data on the base year as this allows for a quicker assessment of which cases have changed the most.

TABLE 2.6
The Alphabet Is Not a Meaningful Variable:
National League Central Standings (7/20/07)

	W	L	Pct	GB
Chicago Cubs	51	44	0.537	3
Cincinatti Reds	41	55	0.427	13.5
Houston Astros	40	55	0.421	14
Milwaukee Brewers	54	41	0.568	—
Pittsburgh Pirates	40	54	0.426	13.5
St. Louis Cardinals	43	49	0.467	9.5

Source: Major League Baseball, MLB.com http://mlb.mlb.com/.

TABLE 2.7
Sort Data on the Most Meaningful Variable

A. Youth Television Watching		B. Youth Television Watching	
	Percent of 9-year-olds who watch more than 5 hours of television per weekday		Percent of 9-year-olds who watch more than 5 hours of televison per weekday
Canada	14.9	United States	21.5
Denmark	6.0	Spain	17.5
Finland	6.1	Canada	14.9
France	5.5	Netherlands	12.6
Germany	4.4	Ireland	11.8
Ireland	11.8	Italy	9.2
Italy	9.2	Finland	6.1
Netherlands	12.6	Denmark	6.0
Spain	17.5	France	5.5
Sweden	4.7	Sweden	4.7
United States	21.5	Germany	4.4

Source: Uri Bronfenburger, et al. *The State of Americans* (New York: Free Press, 1996); qtd. In William Bennett, *The Index of Leading Cultural Indicators* (New York: Broadway Books, 1999), 230.

In table 2.8, the countries are sorted on all three numerical variables in order to highlight the relative position of the United States, but this is generally an inefficient tabular design, as it requires that each country name be repeated three times.

Decimal Places and Rounding

For most purposes, limit the number of decimal places to what is needed to display the data to two or three significant digits. It is usually not necessary to include dollar signs or percentage signs next to the numbers in a table, although this is sometimes done for the first number in a column. Large population counts and government expenditures should be listed in thousands, millions, or billions to retain two or three significant digits without using more than one decimal place. Be aware that the word "billions" can sometimes cause confusion. The Europeans are slowly changing to the American usage, but in the recent past billion meant a "million million" in Europe and a "thousand million" in the United States.

Howard Wainer, a leading authority on tabular presentation, insists that there is no reason to display more than two significant digits in most tabular displays. He would eliminate the decimal points for the poverty and high school graduates data in table 2.9 and report the median family income in thousands of dollars.[3]

TABLE 2.8
Data Sorted on More Than One Variable:
International Mathematics and Science Scores, 2003

4th-grade Math	4th-grade Science	8th-grade Math
Singapore—594	Singapore—565	Singapore—605
Hong Kong—575	Chinese Taipei—551	Hong Kong—586
Japan—565	Japan—543	Chinese Taipei—585
Chinese Taipei—564	Hong Kong—542	Japan—570
Belgium-Flemish—551	**United States—536**	Belgium-Flemish—537
Netherlands—540	Latvia—532	Netherlands—536
Latvia—536	Hungary—530	Hungary—529
Lithuania—534	Russia—526	Latvia—508
Russia—532	Netherlands—525	Russia—508
Hungary—529	Australia—521	Australia—505
United States—518	New Zealand—520	**United States—504**
Cyprus—510	Belgium-Flemish—518	Lithuania—502
Moldova—504	Italy—516	Scotland—498
Italy—503	Lithuania—512	New Zealand—494
Australia—499	Scotland—502	Slovenia—493
New Zealand—493	Moldova—496	Italy—484
Scotland—490	Slovenia—490	Armenia—478
Slovenia—479	Cyprus—480	Norway—461
Armenia—456	Norway—466	Moldova—460
Norway—451	Armenia—437	Cyprus—459
Iran—389	Iran—414	Iran—411
Philippines—358	Philippines—332	Tunisia—410
Morocco—347	Tunisia—314	Morocco—387
Tunisia—339	Morocco—304	Philippines—378

Source: International Association for the Evaluation of Educational Achievement (IEA), Trends in International Mathematics and Science Study (TIMSS), 2003.

I think Wainer goes too far. Presumably, his rule would have Major League Baseball record the Cubs' winning percentage as 54 percent rather than the .537 proportion. It is true that readers will look at the unrounded income data in table 2.9 and, in their minds, round off to thousands, and that the income data are based on estimates that make any conclusion based on differences of less than a thousand dollars practically meaningless. Nevertheless, the unrounded income figures will allow general readers, I think, to more quickly distinguish the income column from the percentage columns and to more easily discern that it is annual income that is being reported. With some exceptions, percentages are usually fine without decimal points and the high school graduates column could probably do without the decimal.

Researchers using correlation and regression analyses commonly display numbers with too many decimal places—presumably to add an aura of scientific precision. They also report far too many statistics in their tables. Again,

TABLE 2.9
Decimals and Rounding:
Income, Poverty, and Education, by Race and Hispanic Origin: 1998

	Median Family Income (thousands)	Median Family Income	Poverty Rate	% High School Graduates
White	$49	$49,023	10.1	84.3
Asian*	53	52,826	12.5	84.7
Hispanic**	30	29,608	25.6	56.1
Black	29	29,404	26.1	77.0

*Asian and Pacific Islander.
**Hispanics may be of any race.
Source: Statistical Abstract, 2000, tables 250, 737, 755.

the purpose seems to be to impress rather than explain, and the effect is to obscure the most important data in the tables. There is no need for any correlation coefficient, R-Square, or standardized regression coefficient to be displayed with more than two decimal places.

Time

The professional education journal, *Phi Delta Kappan*, sponsors an annual poll of public attitudes about the nation's public schools.[4] Every year in numerous tables, their polling report displays data tables with the years going backward, with the most recent year's data in the first column on the left, as shown in table 2.10. Notice how difficult it is to discern whether the trend is increasing or decreasing.

When each vertical column represents a different time period (such as in table 2.4), always display years in adjacent left to right columns. The same principle applies in the case of other ordered categories such as age groups, years of education, temperature ranges, height, or weight: the categories representing the highest values should generally appear on the right of the table.

TABLE 2.10
A Backward Table

"Do you favor or oppose allowing students and parents to choose to attend a private school at public expense?"

	'02	'01	'99	'98	'97	'96	'95
Favor	46	34	39	41	44	44	36
Oppose	52	62	56	55	50	52	61
Don't know	2	4	5	4	6	4	3

Source: Rose and Gallup, *The 34th Annual Phi Delta Kappa/Gallup Poll.*

TABLE 2.11
Time Periods Displayed Vertically

Period (end date)		*Iraq War Coalition Military Fatalities*				
	U.S.	U.K.	Other*	Total	Days	Fatalities per Day
Initial Major Combat (5/1/03)	140	33	0	173	43	4.0
Post-Combat Occupation (6/24/04)	718	27	59	804	424	1.9
Iraqi Sovereignty (1/20/05)	580	25	27	632	216	2.9
After Constitutional Election (12/14/05)	715	13	18	746	318	2.4
After General Election (1/3/07)	933	32	20	985	412	2.4
The "Surge" (7/19/07)	542	29	5	576	168	3.4
Total	3,628	159	129	3,916	1,581	2.5

*Does not include Iraqi forces.
Source: "Iraq Coalition Count," http://icasualties.org/.

Where time series trends are represented in a vertical column, sort so that the most recent year is at the bottom, as in table 2.11.

Most often time is best represented across the columns rather than the rows of the table, but sometimes this principle conflicts with another one: do not mix different units of measure down the columns. Thus in table 2.11, the several different units of measurement are best defined by columns with time represented by the rows of the table.

Consistency

When a paper or report contains more than one table, the formatting ought to be consistent across tables: same fonts, same heading style, and same borders. If the four racial and ethnic categories are displayed as they are in table 2.9, they ought to be sorted in the same order, despite the sorting rule, in similar tables using the same categories.

Combining Tables

While cramming too much data and too many different kinds of data into a single table should be avoided, one should look for opportunities to combine several tables into one.

Table 2.12, derived from Christina Hoff Sommers's book *War against Boys*, nicely summarizes in a single table what could have been presented in six. The basic format used here is ideal for presenting cross-tabular survey data when a single variable is cross-tabulated against several others. Sommers uses these data to make two points. The first is that teachers favor girls over boys. The

TABLE 2.12
Efficient Presentation of Survey Data:
Unpublished AAUW Data from the 1990 Self-Esteem Survey

	Responses by Sex (%)	
	Girls' Perception	Boys' Perception
Who do teachers think are smarter?		
Boys	13	26
Girls	81	69
Other response	5	5
Who do teachers punish more often?		
Boys	92	90
Girls	5	8
Other response	3	2
Who do teachers compliment more often?		
Boys	7	15
Girls	89	81
Other response	5	4
Who do teachers like to be around?		
Boys	12	21
Girls	80	73
Other response	8	6
Who do teachers pay more attention to?		
Boys	33	29
Girls	57	64
Other response	10	7
Who do teachers call on more often?		
Boys	35	36
Girls	57	59
Other response	8	5

Source: Christina Hoff Sommers, *The War against Boys: How Misguided Feminism Is Harming Our Young Men* (Simon and Schuster, 2000), 42.
Original source of data: American Association of University Women. *Greenberg-Lake Full Data Report: Expectation and Aspirations: Gender Roles and Gender Self-Esteem* (Washington, D.C.: AAUW, 1990), 18.

second more subtle point is conveyed in the title: that the American Association of University Women who conducted the original survey (and who sponsored a report arguing that girls are ignored by teachers) suppressed the release of these data.[5] A less argumentative title for the table might have been, "Boys' and Girls' Perceptions of Teachers' Gender Partiality."

Highlighting Comparisons

The purpose of properly sorting the data, correctly arranging the rows and columns, combining what could be multiple tables into one, and other efficiency rules are to allow the reader to quickly grasp the most meaningful comparisons that the data allow. Highlighting critical numbers in a table can serve the same purpose. On the assumption that the data are being presented to a U.S. audience, the U.S. scores in table 2.8 (and in several other tables with international data) are highlighted in bold. Similarly in chapter 6, the numbers in the diagonal of table 6.2 are highlighted to focus readers' attention on the crucial numerical comparisons.

Borders

A common and simple table format is used in most of the tables on these pages. It includes a thin straight border under the column headings and under the main body of data. The table's title is in bold. Putting the headings in bold is advised only if they are very short headings, and not if it is inconsistent with the format for other tables in the report. The tables include only horizontal lines. Partly this is due to the Modern Language Association (MLA) style guidelines that were originally designed for manuscripts prepared with manual typewriters, but there is usually no need for vertical lines.

MLA and the American Psychological Association (APA) style guidelines recommend that table titles be italicized (one of the few recent acknowledgments that manual typewriters are no longer in use) and aligned to the left with the text underlined and that the table number be placed (again aligned to the left) above the title. These style recommendations, however, are for papers that are not in final form, that is, manuscripts that will later be formatted by a publisher. The MLA style guide also specifies that tables (and the text of manuscripts) be double-spaced and that the tables and charts be placed at the end of the manuscript; this is for the convenience of manuscript typesetters and not for readers (and I am perplexed as to how it might be helpful in any case).

Tables, Text, and Audiences

The general purpose of a table is to present numerical information more efficiently than it can be expressed in the text. There are no hard and fast rules stating when a table is appropriate, but a paragraph with more than four or five numbers usually cries out for a table.

Similarly, charts should be used when they can more efficiently convey the ideas about numerical information than a table can. Tables are usually to be preferred to charts when a very precise representation of the numbers is needed. Daily stock quotes and sports statistics are thus rarely presented in bar charts. Time series trend data of more than five time points is generally better displayed in a time series chart than in a table.

One should strive to balance and integrate the tabular presentations with the textual discussion of the numerical evidence. Beware of "orphan tables": tables that are not referenced in the text. Although academic audiences (e.g., your professors) are sometimes impressed by richly detailed tabular presentations (and by dense and impenetrable writing), too many tables and too many numbers may turn off lay readers. A thesis, term paper, or a Department of Education annual report might contain the full tabulation of math and science scores shown in table 2.8, but a letter to a newspaper editor might summarize it all in one sentence: "American fourth and eighth graders scored above average on the most recent international math tests, while students in only four of twenty-four countries scored better than American fourth graders in science."

In writing directed at general audiences, tables should contain the minimum data necessary to support the conclusions presented in the text. More sophisticated audiences, who might draw their own additional conclusions from a table, will appreciate more detail. Baseball fans, for example, are accustomed to scrutinizing all the numbers in a box score to develop insights into the game that are not presented in the accompanying story.

Paul Krugman's *The Conscience of a Liberal* contains several excellent examples of tables formatted for a general audience and the entire work contains only the bare minimum of tabulated data. The data in table 2.13 indicate the probability of graduating from college for students whose families are in the top and bottom quartiles on a measure of socioeconomic status (measured by their parents' income, occupational status, and education) and for students who scored in the top and bottom quartiles of an eighth grade math exam. From these data, Krugman concludes that "rich dumb kids . . . were more likely to graduate from college" than poor smart ones. In modern America, Krugman suggests, inherited class "usually trumps talent."[6]

Note that without the accompanying text to illustrate how the numbers in the table should be read, many readers will misread even the best designed table. When shown only table 2.13, several of my students misread the num-

TABLE 2.13
Percentage of 1988 Eighth Graders Finishing College

	8th Grade Math Score	
Parents' Socioeconomic Status:	*Bottom Quartile*	*Top Quartile*
Bottom Quartile	3	29
Top Quartile	30	74

Sources: National Center for Education Statistics, *The Condition of Education*, 2003, 47; Krugman, *Conscience of a Liberal*, 248.

bers to conclude that rich kids were more likely to score high on the eighth grade math exam. Illustrating how just one number in a table should be read is often a sufficient guide to interpreting a table.

Notes

1. Quoted in Howard Wainer, *Graphic Discovery* (Princeton, N.J.: Princeton University Press, 2005), 9.

2. Gary King, "Replication, Replication," *PS: Political Science and Politics* 28 (September 1995): 443–99.

3. Howard Wainer, "Improving Tabular Display: With NAEP Tables as Examples and Inspirations," *Journal of Educational and Behavioral Statistics* 22 (1997): 1–30. Wainer is also the most persistent critic of "Alabama First!" alphabetical sorting.

4. Lowell C. Rose and Alec M. Gallup, *The 34th Annual Phi Delta Kappa/Gallup Poll of the Public's Attitudes Toward the Public Schools,* 2002, at www.pdkintl.org/kappan/k0209pol.htm.

5. Christina Hoff Sommers, *The War against Boys: How Misguided Feminism Is Harming Our Young Men* (New York: Simon and Schuster, 2000), 42.

6. Paul Krugman, *The Conscience of a Liberal* (New York: W. W. Norton, 2007), 248.

3

Creating Good Charts

Good information design is clear thinking made visible, while bad design is stupidity in action.—Edward Tufte, *Visual Explanations*

A GRAPHICAL CHART PROVIDES a visual display of numerical information that otherwise would be presented in a table: a table, that which otherwise would be presented in text. Ideally, a chart should convey ideas about the data that would not be readily apparent if they were displayed in a table or as text. Designing good charts, however, presents more challenges than tabular display as it draws on the talents of both the scientist and the artist. You have to know and understand your data, but you also need a good sense of how the reader will visualize the chart's graphical elements.

General Principles of Graphic Display

The two standards for tabular design—the *efficient* display of meaningful and *unambiguous* data—apply to charts as well. As with tables, it is crucial to good charting to choose meaningful data, to define precisely what the numbers represent, and to present the data in a manner that allows the reader to quickly grasp what the data mean. Data ambiguity in charts and tables results from the failure to define precisely just what the numbers in the presentation represent. Every dot on a scatterplot, every point on a time series line, every bar on a bar chart represents a number (actually, in the case of a scatterplot, two numbers). It is the job of the chart's text to tell the reader what each of those numbers means.

Two problems arise in charting that are less common in tabular displays. Poor or deliberately deceptive choices in graphic design can provide a distorted picture of numbers and relationships they represent. A more common problem is that charts are often designed in ways that hide what the data might tell us, or that distract the reader from quickly discerning the meaning of the evidence presented in the chart. Two classic texts on the graphical display of numbers: Darrell Huff's *How to Lie with Statistics*[1] and Edward Tufte's *The Visual Display of Quantitative Information*[2] illustrate many of the more common problems.

Huff's little paperback, first published in 1954 and reissued many times thereafter, contained many illustrations of graphical distortions of data such as the "crescive cow" shown in figure 3.1. The height of the cow is proportional to the number of milk cows in the United States, which increased from 8 million in 1860 to 25 million in 1936. The 1936 cow is thus three times the height of the 1860 one, but the graphic is also three times as wide, taking up nine times the area of the page. Moreover, the graphic is a depiction of a three-dimensional figure: when we take the depth of the cow into account, she is twenty-seven times larger in 1936. Later, Tufte developed the "lie factor" statistic: a numerical measure of the data distortion. Here, representing a number that is three times larger in magnitude with an image that is twenty-seven times larger produces a lie factor of nine.

Such visual distortions are not as common as they once were, but modern computer technology has made possible all sorts of new ways of lying with charts.

THE CRESCIVE COW

1860   1936

FIGURE 3.1
Graphical Distortion of Data
From *How to Lie with Statistics* by Darrel Huff illustrated by Irving Gies. Copyright 1954 and renewed © 1982 by Darrell Huff and Irving Gies. Used by permission of W. W. Norton & Company, Inc.

Edward Tufte would second Emperor Joseph II's famous complaint to a young composer: "too many notes, Mozart." Tufte's unique contribution to the art of graphic design was to stress the virtue of efficient data presentation. His fundamental rule of efficient graphical design is to "minimize the ink-to-data ratio" by eliminating any elements from the chart that do not aid in conveying what the numbers mean. Tufte's advice to those who would chart is essentially the same advice offered by William Strunk and E. B. White to would-be writers: "A sentence should contain no unnecessary words, a paragraph no unnecessary sentences for the same reason that a drawing should have no unnecessary lines and a machine no unnecessary parts."[3]

Just as the purpose of any statistic is to simplify, to represent in one number a larger set of numbers, the purpose of a chart is to simplify numerical comparisons: to represent several numerical comparisons in a single graphic. The most common errors in chart design are to include elements in the graphical display that have nothing to do with presenting the numerical comparisons. Below we will see how the standard applies to the components of charts in general.

The Components of a Chart

There are three basic components to most charts: the text, the axes, and the graphical elements. The textual labels: the chart's title, axes titles, axis labels, legends, and notes, define the numbers. The chart's graphical elements: the bars, pie slices, and lines, represent the magnitudes of the numbers. The X and Y axes define the scale of the numbers represented in the chart.

Chart Titles

In journalistic writing, a chart title will sometimes state the conclusion the writer would have the reader draw from the chart ("Stock Market Crashes"). In academic writing, the title should define the data series without imposing a data interpretation on the reader. Often, the units of measurement are specified at the end of the title after a colon, or in parentheses in a subtitle (e.g., "constant dollars," "% of GDP," or "billions of U.S. dollars"). More often than not, titles placed above the chart are centered, while caption titles placed below the chart are left justified. In this chapter, I use both generic figure captions below the charts ("The Components of a Chart,") in figure 3.2, and data-specific charts titles ("Chart Title") centered above the graphic.

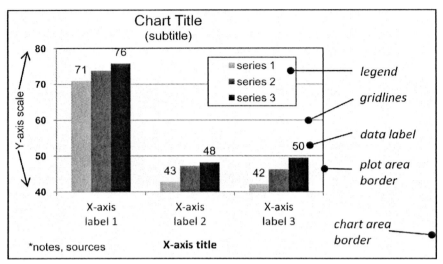

FIGURE 3.2
Components of a Chart

Axis Titles and Labels

Axis titles should be succinct, and not used if they merely repeat what is clear from the main title or axis labels. If a chart title indicates that the data are measured as a "% of GDP," it is not necessary to repeat the wording in the title of the *Y*-axis. Using "Year" as the *X*-axis title in time series charts is redundant when the *X*-axis labels (e.g., "1990, 1991, 1992") clearly represent years.

Axis Scale and Data Labels

The value or magnitude of the main graphical elements of a chart are defined by either or both the axis scale and individual data labels. One should avoid using too many numbers to define the data points. A bar chart with numerical data labels on each individual bar does not need additional numbers on the *Y*-axis. If it seems necessary to have numeric labels for every value in a chart, consider that a table is probably a more efficient way of presenting the data.

Legends

Legends are used when a chart has more than one data series and are usually only needed for bar charts. With time series charts, labeling the actual trendline usually works better than a separate legend and sometimes elimi-nates the need to distinguish the lines with additional markers. If legends are used, they should correspond to the ordering of the graphical elements they represent.

Gridlines

If used at all, gridlines should use as little ink as possible so as not to over-whelm the main graphical elements of the chart.

Sources

Specifying the source of the data is important for proper academic citation, but it can also give knowledgeable readers who are often familiar with com-mon data sources important insights into the reliability and validity of the data. For example, knowing that crime statistics come from the FBI rather than the National Crime Victimization Survey can be a crucial bit of infor-mation.

Other Chart Elements

The amount of ink given over to the nondata elements of a chart that are not necessary for defining the meaning and values of the data should be kept to a minimum. Chart area borders, plot area borders, and chart-and-plot area shading are unnecessary. Keep the shading of the graphical elements simple and avoid the visually distracting diagonal hatching of bars and pie slices. In most of the charts that follow, even the vertical line defining the *Y*-axis has been removed, following the commendable charting standards of the *Econo-mist* magazine. One intriguing *Economist* chart feature, too unconventional for this text, is to place the *Y*-axis on the right-hand side of time series charts, allowing the reader to more readily identify the last, most important, values in the trend.

Three-dimensional bar charts and pie charts are the most unforgivable vi-olation of Tufte's minimize the ink-to-data ratio rule. They are visually dis-tracting, offer a less precise representation of the numbers, make meaningful comparisons of the numbers more difficult, and often produce graphical dis-tortions of the data.

Printed charts should have a primarily white background, but for charts used in slideshows, use a dark (usually blue) background and bright primary colors (white, yellow, red, and light blue) for the text and chart elements.

When Graphic Design Goes Badly

The most general standards of charting data are thus the following:

- Present meaningful data.
- Define the data unambiguously.
- Do not distort the data.
- Present the data efficiently.

To see what happens when these rules are violated, consider figure 3.3 taken from Robert Putnam's *Bowling Alone* (where it was labeled figure 47), a work that contains many good and bad examples of graphical data display (and, unfortunately, no tables at all).[4] In just one chart, Putnam violates all four of the standards: the chart does not depict meaningful data, the data it does depict are ambiguous, the graphical elements distort the data, and the chart design is seriously inefficient.

Of these, let us consider the inefficiency first: the first thing you notice about the chart is the 3-D effect. On both efficiency and truthfulness grounds, this is unfortunate; the 3-D effect is unnecessary and in this case serves to distort the visual representation of the data. Had not the data labels been shown on the top of each bar, it would not be readily apparent that bar A is in fact

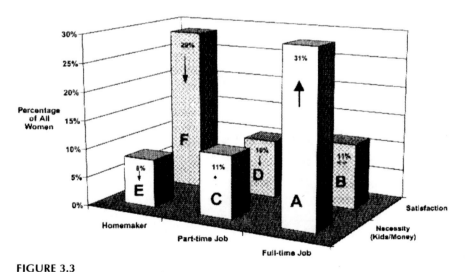

FIGURE 3.3
Very Bad Graphical Display
Source: DDB Needham Life Style Survey Archive, 1978, 1980–1999. Reprinted with permission of Simon and Schuster Adult Publishing Group from *Bowling Alone: The Collapse and Revival of American Community*, by Robert D. Putnam. Copyright © 2000 by Robert D. Putnam.

taller than bar F, or that C is the same size as B. In addition, the chart suffers from "numbering inefficiency": the chart uses thirteen numbers to represent just six data points.

The rotation of the 3-D graphic distorts the size of the bars. Bar A, which represents a number (31%) only 6 percent larger than the number represented by bar F (29%) is at least 20 percent larger than bar F. Eliminating the 3-D, as shown in figure 3.4, offers a more exact representation of the data with a lot less ink.

There are two problems of ambiguous data in Putnam's chart. If one looks at the chart quickly, the first impression one would get is that only 11 percent of women who work full-time do so for reasons of personal satisfaction. But that is not the case. Look at the Y-axis title, or notice that the percentages represented by all six bars add up to one hundred. Of all the women in the survey, 11 percent were in the single category of "employed full-time for reasons of personal satisfaction." This is resolved in Putnam's text, where he explains that bar E is the percentage of all women who are homemakers out of concern for their kids while bar A is the percentage of all women who are working full-time because they need the money. This is not what readers normally expect in a bar chart, but given the data Putnam has decided to display, there is not a whole lot that can be done to fix it.

The second ambiguity has to do with the part-time category. Are women not working full-time out of concern for the kids or are they not staying at home full-time out of concern for the kids?

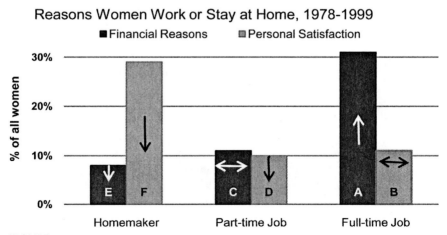

FIGURE 3.4
Revised Chart, without 3-D Effects

Still, we have to ask, "What does this chart mean?" In particular, what data do the arrows on the bars represent?

A critical standard of good charting is that the chart should be self-explanatory. That there are problems with this chart becomes apparent to the reader as soon as one encounters Putnam's page and a half of accompanying text devoted, not to explaining the significance of the data, but to explaining what the elements of the chart represent. A careful reading of the text tells us that there are three conclusions Putnam would have us draw from this chart:

- Over time (the 1980s and 1990s), more women are working.
- They are doing so less for reasons of personal satisfaction and more out of necessity (i.e., to earn money).
- Correspondingly, there has been a significant decline in the number of women who choose to be homemakers for reasons of personal satisfaction.

These three conclusions are directly relevant to Putnam's general thesis: that over time there has been a decline in social capital (adults are spending less time raising children and developing the social capital of future generations) driven in part by the demands of the expanding workforce.

Based on the textual discussion that Putnam offers it becomes clear that the most meaningful data are represented in the chart, not by the height of the bars, but by the direction of the arrows on the bars. Generally, data presentations that include more than one time point provide for much more meaningful analyses than cross-sectional or single time point presentations. Although most of the data analysis in *Bowling Alone* is time series data, in this case Putnam averages twenty-one years of data down to single data points represented by the chart's bars, with the time series change represented by arrows. Thus, the most meaningful comparison in the chart—the comparison that support the conclusion that Putnam seeks to draw from the data—is not that bar A is higher than bar B or F, but that the arrow for bar A is going up while the arrow for bar F is going down. The height of the bars is irrelevant to any conclusion Putnam draws from the data.

The crucial comparison is made directly in figure 3.5, based on the data presented in the textual discussion. Moreover, it directly illustrates several points that neither the text nor the original chart make clear: In 1978, a plurality of women were homemakers who did so out of personal satisfaction. In 1999, women who worked full-time for financial reasons were the plurality.

Figure 3.5 also eliminates the ambiguous part-time category and clarifies that "necessity" refers to "kids" in the case of homemakers and to "money" in the case of full-time workers.

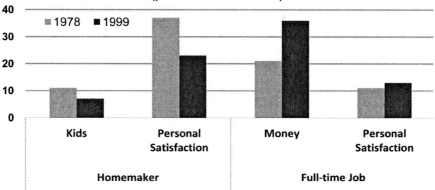

FIGURE 3.5
Revised Chart, with Data from Text
Source: Putnam, *Bowling Alone*, 197–98.

Types of Charts

Most charts are a variation on one of four basic types: pie charts, bar charts, time series charts, and scatterplots. Choosing the right type of chart depends on the characteristics of the data and the relationships you want to display.

Pie Charts

Pie charts represent the distribution of the categorical components of a single variable. Generally, comparisons of rates are more meaningful than variable distributions and for this and other reasons pie charts should be used rarely, if at all.

Pie charts also contain more ink than is necessary to display the data and the slices provide for a poor representation of the magnitude of the data

---

Rules for Pie Charts

- Avoid using pie charts.
- Use pie charts only for data that add up to some meaningful total.
- Never ever use three-dimensional pie charts; they are even worse than two-dimensional ones.
- Avoid forcing comparisons across more than one pie chart.

Federal Government Receipts by Source: 2000 - 2007

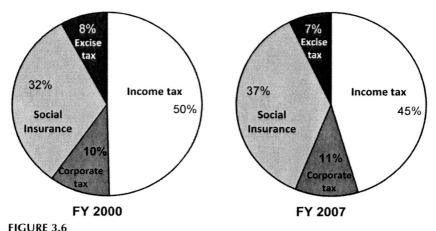

FIGURE 3.6
Comparing Two Pie Charts
Source: Budget of the United States Government, 2007. Historical Tables, table 2.1.

points. If pie charts are used, the purpose should be to compare a single slice of the pie to the whole, not to compare two slices to each other. Do you remember as a kid trying to decide which slice of your birthday cake was the largest? It is more difficult for the eye to discern the relative size of pie slices than it is to assess relative bar length. Forcing the reader to draw comparisons across the two pie charts shown in figure 3.6 is also a bad idea: without looking at the data label percentages in the figures, one cannot easily determine whether the FY 2000 slices are larger or smaller than the corresponding FY 2007 slices.

Three-dimensional pies are even worse, as they also add a visual distortion of the data. In figure 3.7, the thick 3-D band exaggerates the size of the corporate income tax slice. Exploding 3-D pie charts are for decoration, not data analysis.

A simple bar chart, shown in figure 3.8, will convey all the information in the pie charts more precisely and with far less ink.

Nevertheless, people like pie charts. Readers expect to see one or two pie charts similar to those in figure 3.6 at the very beginning of an annual agency budget report, but it would be a mistake to rely on several pie charts for the primary data analysis in a report.

For those who would ignore all the advice given here and insist that good charts must look pretty, the most recent version of the Microsoft Excel® charting software (in Office 2007) will satisfy all your foolish desires. It features

Federal Government Receipts by Source: 2000

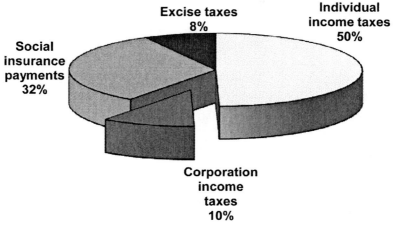

FIGURE 3.7
Exploding 3-D Pie Chart

Source of Federal Government Receipts
(billions of current dollars)

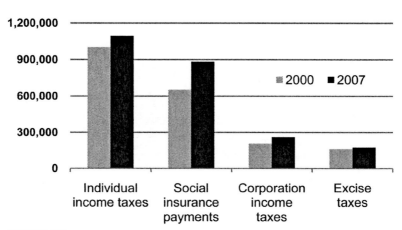

FIGURE 3.8
Bar Charts Are Better Than Pie Charts

3-D pie charts that gleam and glisten like Christmas tree ornaments, to say nothing about what you can do with the 3-D pie chart's pretty but also pretty useless cousins: the donut, cylinder, cone, radar, and pyramid charts.

One interesting variation on pie charting does offer an excellent visual representation of certain kinds of data and is similar to the product evaluation charts shown in *Consumer Reports*. Figure 3.9 is a revised version of a chart that appeared in the *Economist* in the 1980s when countries across the world were beginning to privatize government-owned sectors of the economy.[5]

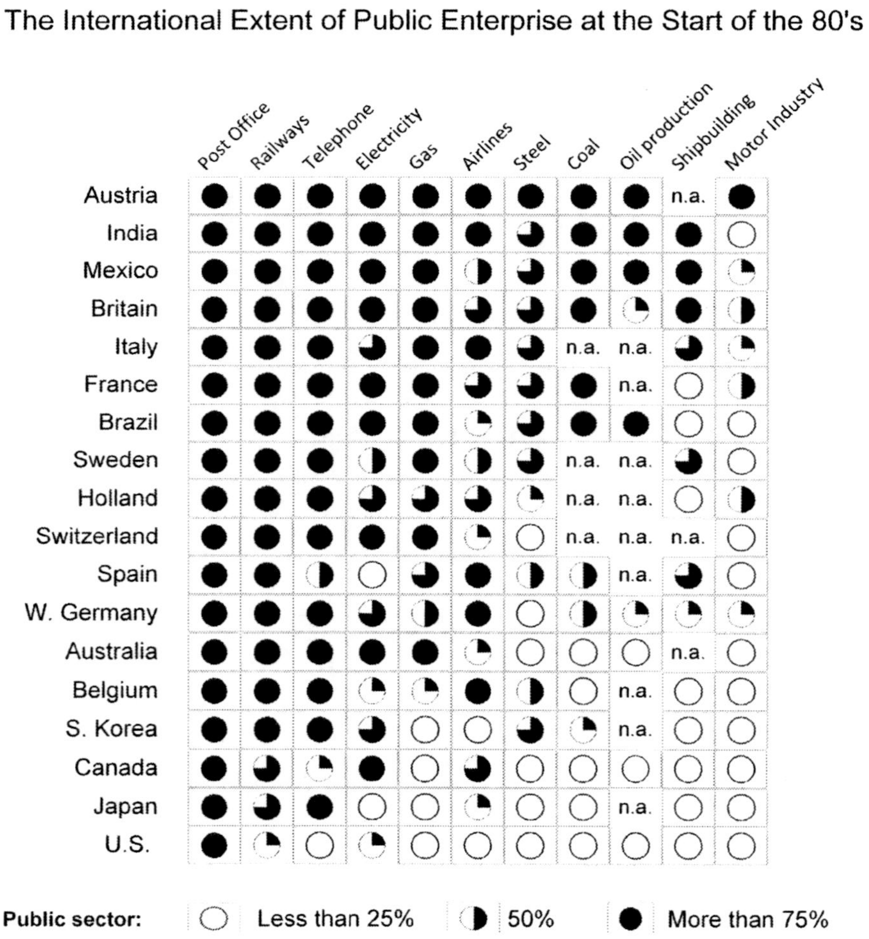

The International Extent of Public Enterprise at the Start of the 80's

	Post Office	Railways	Telephone	Electricity	Gas	Airlines	Steel	Coal	Oil production	Shipbuilding	Motor Industry
Austria	●	●	●	●	●	●	●	●	●	n.a.	●
India	●	●	●	●	●	●	◕	●	●	●	○
Mexico	●	●	●	●	●	◐	◕	●	●	●	◕
Britain	●	●	●	●	●	◕	◕	●	◕	●	◐
Italy	●	●	●	◕	●	●	◕	n.a.	n.a.	◕	◔
France	●	●	●	●	●	◕	◕	●	n.a.	○	◐
Brazil	●	●	●	●	●	◔	◕	●	●	○	○
Sweden	●	●	●	◐	●	◕	◕	n.a.	n.a.	◕	○
Holland	●	●	●	◕	◕	◕	◔	n.a.	n.a.	○	◐
Switzerland	●	●	●	●	●	◔	○	n.a.	n.a.	n.a.	○
Spain	●	●	◐	○	◕	●	◐	◐	n.a.	◕	○
W. Germany	●	●	●	◕	◐	●	○	◐	◔	◔	◔
Australia	●	●	●	●	●	◔	○	○	○	n.a.	○
Belgium	●	●	●	◔	◔	●	◐	○	n.a.	○	○
S. Korea	●	●	●	◕	○	○	◕	◔	n.a.	○	○
Canada	●	◕	◔	●	○	◕	○	○	○	○	○
Japan	●	◕	●	○	○	◔	○	○	n.a.	○	○
U.S.	●	◔	○	◔	○	○	○	○	○	○	○

Public sector: ○ Less than 25%   ◑ 50%   ● More than 75%

FIGURE 3.9
Pie Charts on a Guttman Scale
Source: "Privatisation," *Economist*, 12/21/1985, 72.

When the data are sorted (the original *Economist* presentation was sorted alphabetically) so that the countries with the most publicly held industries are at the top and the industries most commonly publicly held at the left, the tabulation forms a Guttman Scale, allowing one to quickly discern the relative extent of public ownership across countries and industries.

Bar Charts

Bar charts typically display the relationship between one or more categorical variables with one or more quantitative variables represented by the length of the bars. The categorical variables are usually defined by the categories displayed on the *X*-axis and, if there is more than one data series, by the legend.

Bar charts are not a very efficient method of data presentation and often contain little data, a lot of ink, and rarely reveal ideas that cannot be presented much more simply in a table. Minimizing the ink-to-data ratio is especially important in the case of bar charts. Never use a 3-D bar chart. Keep the gridlines faint. Display no more than seven numbers on the *Y*-axis scale. If there are fewer than five bars, consider using data labels rather than a *Y*-axis scale; it doesn't make sense to use a five-numbered *Y*-axis scale when the exact values can be shown with four numbers.

As with tables, sorting the data on the most significant variable greatly eases the interpretation of the data. The data in figure 3.10 are sorted on the child rather than the elderly poverty rates only because most of the research on the topic has focused on child poverty. Note also that if the sorted variable represents time, time should always go from left to right and on the *X*-axis.

Look at figure 3.10 and you can quickly grasp the main points—the United States has the highest child poverty rate among developed nations—but spend some time with it and you will discover other interesting things. Note, for example, the differences in child and elderly poverty across nations or that the three countries at the top, with the lowest child poverty rates are Scandinavian countries. Five of the seven countries with the highest child poverty are English-language countries.

Rules for Bar Charts

- Minimize the ink; do not use 3-D effects.
- Sort the data on the most significant variable.
- Use rotated bar charts if there are more than eight to ten categories.
- Place legends inside or below the plot area.
- With more than one data series, beware of scaling distortions.

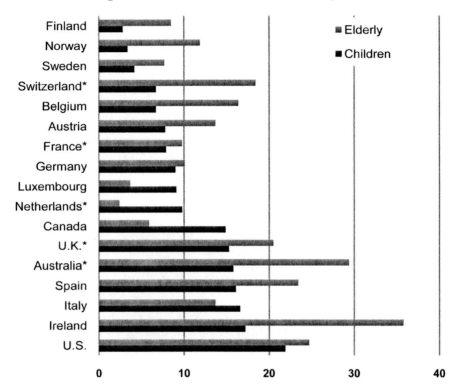

Relative Poverty Rates in Wealthy Nations, 2000
% living in families below 50% of median family income

* most recent year

FIGURE 3.10
Rotated Bar Chart with Two Data Series
Source: Luxembourg Income Study, http://www.lisproject.org/keyfigures.htm.

One variation of the bar chart, the stacked bar chart, should be used with caution, especially when there is no implicit order to the categories that make up the bar (i.e., when the categorical variable is nominal rather than ordinal), as is the case in figure 3.11. Note how difficult it is to compare the differences in the size of the components across the upper parts of two bars. The same difficulty occurs with "stacked" line and area charts.

The stacked bar chart works best when the primary comparisons are to be made across the data series represented at the bottom of the bar. Thus, placing the "teachers" data series at the bottom of the bars in figure 3.12 (and

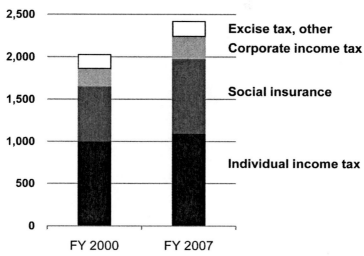

Federal Government Receipts, 2000-2007
(Billions of current dollars)

Excise tax, other

Corporate income tax

Social insurance

Individual income tax

FY 2000   FY 2007

FIGURE 3.11
Stacked Bar Chart with Nominal Categories

Educational Staffing by Function in Selected Countries: 1995

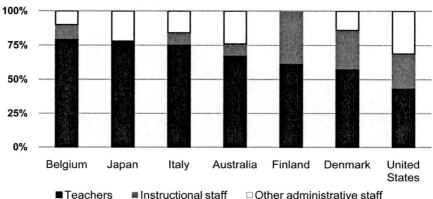

Belgium Japan Italy Australia Finland Denmark United States

■ Teachers   ▨ Instructional staff   □ Other administrative staff

FIGURE 3.12
Stacked (100%) Bar Chart
Source: OECD, Education at a Glance, 1995.

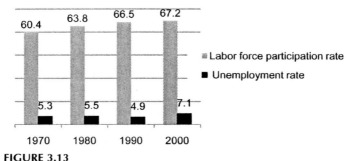

FIGURE 3.13
Scaling Effects in a Bar Chart with Two Data Series
Source: U.S. Statistical Abstract, 2001, CD-ROM, table 567.

sorting the data on that series) forces the reader's attention on the crucial comparison and the obvious conclusion: American teachers enjoy the luxury of having a large supervisory and support staff.

One common bar chart mistake is to include the legend on the right-hand side of the plot area, allowing the text to shrink the space devoted to the graphic representation (see figure 3.13). Placing the legend inside the plot area, as in figure 3.10, or horizontally under the table title, as in figure 3.12, maximizes the size of the area given over to displaying the data.

Potentially misleading scaling effects occur when a bar chart (or a line chart, as we will see) has two data series with numbers of a substantially different magnitude, minimizing the variation in the data series containing the smaller numbers. Figure 3.13, for example, depicts the increase in the labor force participation rate (the percentage of the adult population in the labor force) from 60 percent in 1970 to 67 percent in 2000, and the increase in the unemployment rate from 5.3 percent to 7.1 percent. The immediate visual impression the chart gives is that the labor force participation rate is larger than the unemployment rate (a relatively meaningless comparison) and that labor force participation is growing, while the important variation in the unemployment rate (a 30 percent increase) is hardly noticeable. Including an additional bar representing the sum of the other bars in a chart (as shown in figure 3.14) has the same effect of reducing the variation in the main graphical elements.

To see what happens when bar charting rules are violated, consider the example in figure 3.15, taken from an annual report of the Illinois Board of Higher Education (IBHE—conflict of interest disclosure: my employer).

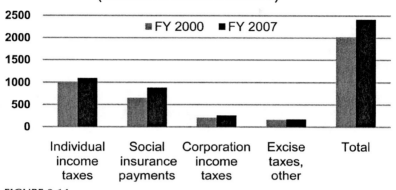

Source of Federal Government Receipts
(billions of current dollars)

FIGURE 3.14
Scaling Effect in a Bar Chart
Source: U.S. Budget, Historical Tables.

Total 12-Month Headcounts

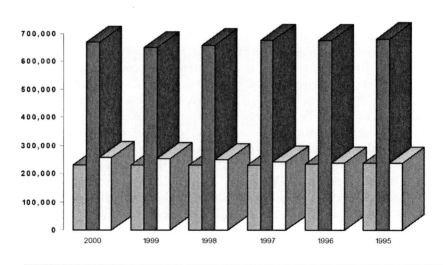

FIGURE 3.15
A Really Bad Bar Chart
Source: Illinois Board of Higher Education, Illinois Higher Education Annual Report (July 2002), 24.

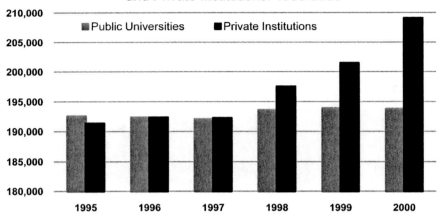

FIGURE 3.16
Revised Enrollment Chart
Source: Illinois Board of Higher Education, Data Book, 2004.

There is more wrong with this chart than just the 3-D effect. Look carefully at the *X*-axis and notice the year 2000 on the far left. Notice also, how flat the trends are. Even if time were going the right way, it is not easy to tell which trend is increasing or decreasing.

By using comparable data (the only available data: Fall semester head-counts rather than twelve-month headcounts), eliminating the 3-D effects, sorting time from left to right, removing the community college data series, and adjusting the bottom of the scale, we see something in figure 3.16 that the IBHE chart obscured. Private institution enrollments are increasing while public university enrollments are flat. Here, there is reason to believe that the data deception, if not intentional, is at least self-serving. It is within the scope of the IBHE's responsibility to advocate that public universities increase their enrollments, but the Board has been quiet. That these enrollment trends serve the interests of both the private and public institutions more than they serve the public interest may have something to do with that.

There is some debate among charting enthusiasts as to whether charts should include zero as the base for the *Y*-axis. Critics of not using a zero-base insist that reducing the scale, as in figure 3.16, exaggerates the variation in the data. Here, the private institutions' bar for 2000 is more than twice as high as the public university bar, but the private institution enrollments are only about 8 percent higher. The "lie factor" is fourteen. Jane E. Miller argues that

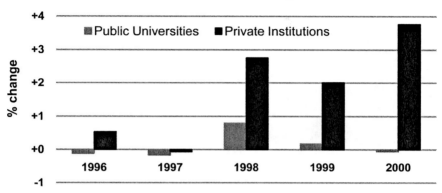

FIGURE 3.17
Bar Chart with Annual Change Data

Y-axis scales should start at zero with "rare exceptions" (none of her charts is an exception).[6] Howard Wainer, however, insists that any choice of scale is arbitrary. "Automatic rules," he says, "do not always work; wisdom and honesty are always required."[7] The downside of using the zero-base is that it can hide significant variations in the data. I do not think that the depiction in figure 3.16 is at all unfair. It is fair to say, I think, that private institutions have accounted for most of the growth in university and college enrollments in the state, and the graph shows that well. Miller suggests that calculating annual change and using a zero-base would be preferable, but as we see in figure 3.17, this exaggerates the differences even more.

Histograms are a form of bar chart used to display the distribution of a continuous variable along a set of defined categorical ranges. The histogram in figure 3.18 provides a graphic depiction of the segregation of black and Hispanic students in Illinois public schools. If there were very little segregation, most of the schools would have between 30 percent and 50 percent of student body black or Hispanic. Instead, over half of the state's approximately 3,200 schools have a student body that is either more than 90 percent, or less than 10 percent, black or Hispanic.

Time Series Line Charts

The time series chart is one of the most efficient means of displaying large amounts of data in ways that provide for meaningful analysis.

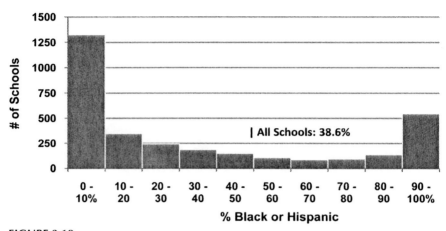

Illinois Public Schools, Racial and Ethnic Compositon, 2006

FIGURE 3.18
A Histogram
Source: Illinois State Board of Education, 2006 Illinois Report Card Data file.

Rules for time series (line) charts:

- Time is always displayed on the X-axis from left to right.
- Display as much data with as little ink as possible.
- Make sure the reader can clearly distinguish the lines for separate data series.
- Beware of scaling effects.
- When displaying fiscal or monetary data over time, it is often best to use deflated data (e.g., inflation-adjusted or % of GDP).

Time series data are often used to highlight important societal and political trends. In their 1976 book, *The Changing American Voter,* Norman Nie, Sidney Verba, and John Petrocik cited the steady decline in new voters affiliating with either political party (see chapter 1, figure 1.2) as evidence of the increasing sophistication of the electorate.[8]

One should always be cautious in predicting the future from time series trends alone—the predictions of future global warming are based not only on the direction of recent temperature trends (figure 1.2) but on scientific analysis of the things that are causing the warming. Stock market analysts have a saying: "The trend is not your friend." If the trend line in figure 3.19 were a stock price, now would be a good time to sell. The mere passage of time does

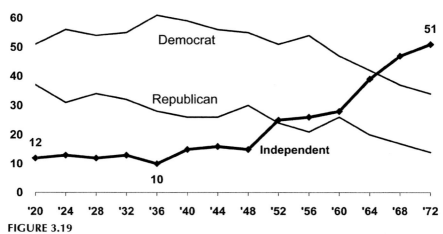

Party Identification of Age Cohorts at Entrance into the Electorate, 1920-1972

FIGURE 3.19
A Time Series Trend
Nie, Verba, and Petrocik, *The Changing American Voter*, 78.

not cause trends to go up or down. Independent voting increased because something else happened. Either the parties changed or the voters did.

Scaling Effects

When two variables with numbers of different magnitudes are graphed on the same chart, the variable with the larger scale will generally appear to have a greater degree of variation. The smaller-scale variable will appear relatively "flat" even though the percentage change is the same. In figure 3.20, ABCorp's stock seems to be growing much faster than XYZ.com's, yet the rate of increase is identical.

One solution to graphical scaling distortions is to use a logarithmic *Y*-axis scale. On a log scale, trendlines of different magnitudes that have the same percentage increase will display the same increase in the height of the trendline, as we see with the same data graphed in figure 3.21.

Log scales often work well with time series data that tends to increase or decrease at a consistent percentage rate, such as prices (in current rather than constant dollars) and population counts (for example, counts of poor persons rather than the poverty rate). Trends in many such variables often display a

Chapter 3

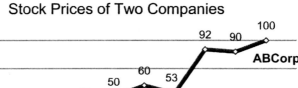

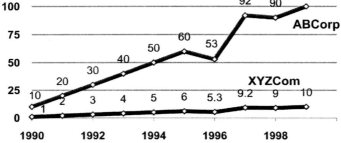

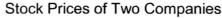

FIGURE 3.20
Illustration of Scaling Distortion
(Hypothetical data)

pattern very similar to what we see in figure 3.22. The chart leaves the visual impression that government outlays (spending) have barely grown for half a century and are now rapidly accelerating.

Comparing the federal outlays in figure 3.22 to the logged scale in figure 3.23, we find that federal outlays in recent decades have actually increased at about the same percentage rate as they did in earlier decades. What appeared to be dramatic accelerations in spending are relatively minor changes compared to those that occurred during World War I and II.

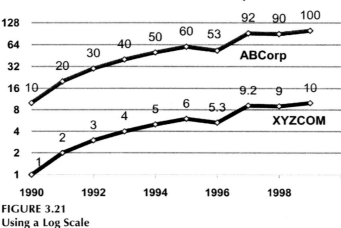

FIGURE 3.21
Using a Log Scale

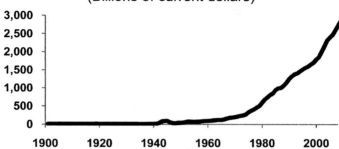

FIGURE 3.22
Trend with Fixed-Unit Scale
Source: Budget of the United States Government, 2007. Historical Tables, table 1.1.

Nevertheless, unless one is writing for an audience of seismologists, log scales should be used cautiously. The statistically illiterate will not care what scale is used, but the statistically semiliterate are likely to take exception to log scale and to view them as an attempt at data distortion. In most cases, using some form of ratio measure is a better solution. In the case of the federal government outlays measure, a measure of outlays per capita, in constant dollars (e.g., adjusted for inflation) or outlays as a percentage of GDP would be preferable alternatives.

When two variables that are measured in different units (say, dollars and rates), or when the differences in scale are so great as to eliminate most of

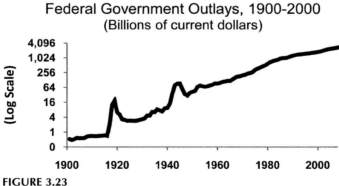

FIGURE 3.23
Trend with Log Scale

the perceived variation in the smaller-scale variable, a second scale, displayed on the right-hand side as in figure 3.24, is sometimes preferable. On the down side, this may make the interpretation of the graph more complicated.

During the 1992 presidential election, the Clinton campaign slogan, "It's the economy, stupid," reflected the general conventional wisdom (and political science research) that economy drives the public's evaluation of the job performance of elected officials.[9] President George W. Bush's record since the beginning of the Iraq War—a steadily improving economy (marked by declining unemployment) and a steadily declining approval rating—is a most notable exception.

Many who have written about graphical distortion condemn the use of two-scale charts because the relative sizes of the two scales are completely arbitrary. This is true: if job approval and unemployment were plotted on the same 0 to 90 *Y*-axis scale, the unemployment rate would be an almost flat line at the bottom of the chart. Again, wisdom and honesty should be the rule.

Scatterplots

The two-dimensional scatterplot is the most efficient medium for the graphical display of data. A simple scatterplot will tell you more about the re-

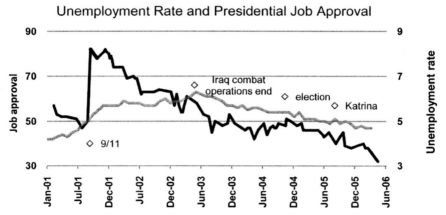

Job approval: "How would you rate President Bush's performance on the job?" (% excellent or good)

FIGURE 3.24
Time Series Chart with Second *Y*-Axis and Annotations
Source: Zogby International (special feature), http://www.zogby.com/features/zogbytables4.cfm; Unemployment: Bureau of Labor Statistics: http://www.bls.gov/cps/.

Rules for Scatterplots
- Use two interval-level variables.
- Fully define the variables with the axis titles.
- Use the chart title to identify both variables and the units of analysis (e.g., people, cities, or states).
- If there is an implied causal relationship between the variables, place the independent variable (the one that causes the other) on the *X*-axis and the dependent variable (the one that may be caused by the other) on the *Y*-axis.
- Scale the axes to maximize the use of the plot area for displaying the data points.
- If possible, use data labels rather than dots to identify the cases.

lationship between two continuous (or interval-level) variables than any other method of presenting or summarizing such data.

With good labeling of the variables and cases and commonsense scaling of the *X* and *Y* axes, there is not a lot that can go wrong with a scatterplot, although extreme outliers on one or more of the variables can obscure patterns in the data.

Figure 3.25 depicts the relationship between Robert Putnam's social capital index, a measure of citizen engagement in public affairs, and state political

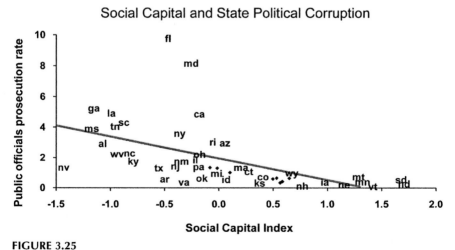

FIGURE 3.25
Scatterplot with Data Labels and Trendline
Sources: Schlesinger and Meier, "Targeting Political Corruption"; Putnam, *Bowling Alone* website http://www.bowlingalone.com/data.htm.

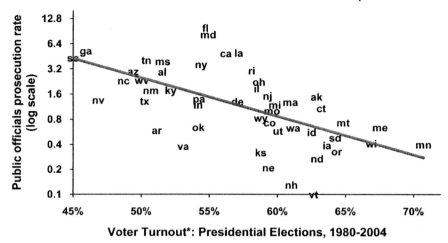

*votes cast/voting eligible population

FIGURE 3.26
Scatterplot with Log-Scaled Y-Axis
Source: Turnout: U.S. Elections Project: http://elections.gmu.edu.

corruption, measured by the rate of prosecutions of public officials, as reported in a study by Thomas Schlesinger and Kenneth Meier.[10] Often scatterplots represent each case on the chart with a single point, but labeling the points conveys much more information, as is done here with the state postal codes. Figure 3.25 also includes a linear trendline, based on a bivariate regression equation, although in this case the relationship appears to be curvilinear.

Sometimes, when the relationship between two variables is not linear or when one of the variables is highly skewed (e.g., with a few cases with relatively high values), a log scale offers a better picture of the relationship. In figure 3.26, using voter turnout as the X-axis variable, the prosecution rate variable is scaled on a logged Y-axis. Log-scaled scatterplots are commonly used with cross-national data where a few very wealthy nations tend to have very high scores on many variables.

Boxplots

John W. Tukey invented the boxplot as a convenient method of displaying the distribution of interval-level variables.

Rules for Boxplots

- A simple boxplot plots the median and four quartiles of data for an interval-level variable.
- Boxplots are best used for comparing the distribution of the same variable for two or more groups or two or more time points.
- Boxplots are an excellent means of displaying how a single case compares to a large number of other cases.

The simple boxplot in figure 3.27 displays the four quartiles of the data, with the "box" comprising the two middle quartiles, separated by the median. Single lines extending above and below the box represent the upper and lower quartiles. More detailed versions of the boxplot restrict the "whiskers" on the plot to 1.5 times the size of the boxes and plot the higher or lower values (outliers) as individual points. Some versions also plot the mean in addition to the median.

A single boxplot, as in figure 3.27, reveals much less about a data distribution than does a histogram. This is especially so in the case of distributions that are not concentrated around the median, as was the case with the school segregation data in figure 3.18. Note that figure 3.26 is based on the same data as figure 3.18, but says much less about what is going on. The real advantage of the boxplot graphic comes through when several boxplots are used to compare the distribution of a variable across groups or over time. An especially useful elaboration of the boxplot chart is to plot one or a few cases over the boxplot to compare single case to the overall distribution as is done in figure 3.28.

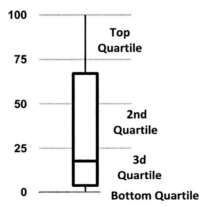

FIGURE 3.27
Components of a Boxplot

Chapter 3

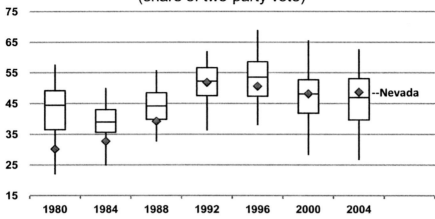

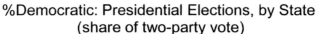

FIGURE 3.28
Comparing Boxplots with Labels for Individual Cases: Nevada
Source: U.S. Statistical Abstract, 2005, CD-Rom, table 388.

Thus, figure 3.28 displays the Democratic vote percentage for the fifty states over the past seven presidential elections. Labeling a single case, we can see that the Democratic vote in Nevada has moved steadily higher relative to the other states. One can easily imagine applying the same plotting strategy in a variety of other settings, for example, comparing one school district's test scores to the distribution of test scores across other school districts.

Sparklines

Edward Tufte's sparkline plots, which he describes as "intense, simple, word-sized graphics," illustrate his principles of graphic minimalism.[11] Sparklines eliminate all the nondata graphical elements of the chart, providing a simply display of the variation in the trend and just enough numerical information to make meaningful comparisons. In figure 3.29, this allows for an efficient comparison of seven economic indicators.

Notes on Microsoft Excel® Charting

All of the charts shown in the book were prepared using the 2007 version of the Microsoft Excel spreadsheet program and some free, downloadable add-ins to the Excel charting software. The 2007 version includes some im-

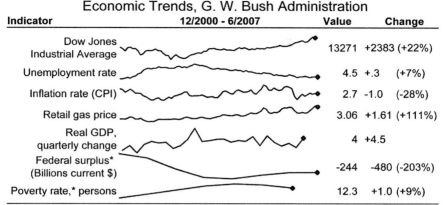

Indicator	Economic Trends, G. W. Bush Administration 12/2000 - 6/2007	Value	Change
Dow Jones Industrial Average		13271	+2383 (+22%)
Unemployment rate		4.5	+.3 (+7%)
Inflation rate (CPI)		2.7	-1.0 (-28%)
Retail gas price		3.06	+1.61 (+111%)
Real GDP, quarterly change		4	+4.5
Federal surplus* (Billions current $)		-244	-480 (-203%)
Poverty rate,* persons		12.3	+1.0 (+9%)

* annual, 2000-2007

FIGURE 3.29
Sparklines
Sources: DJIA: Yahoo! Finance, http://finance.yahoo.com/; unemployment, Inflation: The U.S. Misery Index, http://www.miseryindex.us/; Gas prices: Energy Information Administration, http://tonto.eia.doe.gov/; Surplus: U.S. Budget Historical Tables; Poverty: Census Bureau, Poverty Historical Tables; GDP: Bureau of Economic Analysis, National Accounts.

provements over the earlier 2003 version and some features of some of the charts take advantage of those improvements. Several of the time series charts use wider lines than were possible in Excel 2003 and the log-scaling features, shown in figures 3.21, 3.23, and 3.26, are not easily replicated in the older version.

Two charting applications should have been included in the new version of Excel but were not. Boxplots are not a predefined Excel chart option and require some complicated work-arounds. Fortunately, Jon Peltier has created a downloadable Box and Whisker Chart utility that automates the boxploting process.[12] Most disappointing, the new version of Excel did not include the chart labeling features necessary to include the state abbreviations on the scatterplots in figures 3.25 and 3.26. There are several chart labeling macros and add-ins available on the Internet that add this functionality to the Excel software. The one used here was John Walkenbach's J-Walk Chart Tools.[13] The labeling feature was also used in some of the other charts to control the placement of notations (as in figure 3.13) and to create the uneven X-axis labeling effect shown later in figure 6.1.

All the spreadsheets containing the charts and data shown in this book, with links to the original sources and some advice on using the Excel charting software, are available on the Just Plain Data Analysis website at lilt.ilstu.edu/JPDA/.

Recommended Reading on Charting and Graphic Design

Cleveland, William S. *Visualizing Data.* Summit, N.J.: Hobart Press, 1993.

———. *The Elements of Graphing Data.* Summitt, N.J.: Hobart Press, 1994.

Few, Stephen. *Show Me the Numbers: Designing Tables and Graphs to Enlighten.* Oakland, Calif.: Analytics Press, 2004.

Jones, Gerald E. *How to Lie with Charts.* iUniverse.com, 2000.

Kosslyn, Stephen M. *Elements of Graph Design.* New York: W. H. Freeman, 1994.

Miller, Jane E. "Creating Effective Charts." In *The Chicago Guide to Writing about Numbers,* chapter 7. Chicago, Ill.: University of Chicago Press, 2004.

Tufte, Edward R. *The Visual Display of Quantitative Information.* Cheshire, Conn.: Graphics Press, 1983.

———. *Visual Explanations—Images and Quantities, Evidence and Narrative.* Cheshire, Conn.: Graphics Press, 1997.

Wainer, Howard. *Visual Revelations: Graphical Tales of Fate and Deception from Napoleon Bonaparte to Ross Perot.* Mahwah, N.J.: Lawrence Erlbaum, 1997.

———. *Graphic Discovery.* Princeton, N.J.: Princeton University Press, 2005.

———. *The Second Watch: Navigating in an Uncertain World.*: Princeton, N.J.: Princeton University Press, 2008 (forthcoming).

Walkenbach, John. *Excel Charts.* New York: Wiley, 2002.

Wallgren, Anders, Britt Wallgren, Rolf Persson, Ulf Jorner, and Jan-Aage Haaland. *Graphing Statistics & Data.* Thousand Oaks, Calif.: Sage Publications, 1996.

Notes

1. Darrell Huff, *How to Lie with Statistics* (New York: W. W. Norton, 1993).

2. Edward Tufte, *The Visual Display of Quantitative Information* (Cheshire, Conn.: Graphics Press, 1983).

3. William Strunk and E. B. White, *The Elements of Style* (New York: Macmillan, 1972), 25.

4. Robert D. Putnam, *Bowling Alone* (New York: Simon and Schuster, 2000).

5. "Privatisation," *Economist,* December 21, 1985, 72.

6. Jane E. Miller, *The Chicago Guide to Writing about Numbers* (Chicago, Ill.: University of Chicago Press, 2004), 160.

7. Howard Wainer, *Visual Revelations, Graphical Tales of Fate and Deception from Napoleon Bonaparte to Ross Perot* (Mahwah, N.J.: Lawrence Erlbaum, 1997), 27.

8. Norman H. Nie, Sidney Verba, and John R. Petrocik, *The Changing American Voter* (Cambridge, Mass.: Harvard University Press, 1979).

9. The political science research supporting the "it's the economy, stupid" theory is best summarized in Edward Tufte's *Political Control of the Economy* (Princeton, N.J.: Princeton University Press, 1978).

10. Thomas Schlesinger and Kenneth J. Meier, "The Targeting of Political Corruption in the United States," in *Political Corruption,* Arnold Heidenheimer and Michael Johnston, 3rd ed. (New Brunswick, N.J.: Transaction Publishers, 2002), 627–44.

11. Edward Tufte, *Beautiful Evidence* (Cheshire, Conn.: Graphics Press, 2006), 7–25.

12. Jon Peltier, "Box and Whisker Plots," Peltier Technical Services, Inc., at peltiertech.com/Excel/Charts/BoxWhisker.html.

13. John Walkenbach, "J-Walk Chart Tools," at www.j-walk.com/ss/excel/files/charttools.htm.

4

Voting and Elections

A low voter turnout is an indication of fewer people going to the polls.—
Dan Quayle

VOTER TURNOUT, THE PERCENT OF A POPULATION that turns out to vote, is a
commonly used indicator of the health of a society's democracy and the
level of civic engagement in public affairs. High rates of voter turnout are often
cited as an indicator of public confidence in democratic institutions. In December 2005, for example, the Bush administration enthusiastically trumpeted
the 80 percent turnout (as a percentage of registered voters) in Iraq's first parliamentary elections as a measure of popular support for democracy.[1] Political
commentators often cite voter turnout as an indicator of either the strength of
a society's political culture or the quality of its political institutions. An in-
formed and engaged citizenry that embraces shared values and common interests is more likely to participate in elections. A political system that is responsive to voter interests, that offers voters meaningful choices in contested
elections, and that welcomes open and broad-based political participation offers citizens greater incentives to participate in elections.

Often, low voter turnout and bad government go hand in hand, as we saw
in the relationship between voter turnout and political corruption in chapter
3 (figure 3.26). Entrenched political machines often flourish in a low turnout
political environment where they can mobilize cadres of supporters and
clients to assure safe reelection. Barriers to voting often serve the interests of
incumbent politicians whose positions are at greater risk when new voters
turn out at the polls.

For many who study voting behavior, variations in the rates of voter turnout across various social and demographic groups are a critical aspect of a nation's democratic culture. Who participates in elections often determines who benefits from the election outcomes. Because the elderly, the wealthy, and the better educated generally have higher rates of voting, increasing voter turnout usually requires increasing the participation of young, poor, and less educated voters. In theory, political systems with low voter turnout will be less responsive to the needs of society's "have nots" and more responsive to the interests of those with power.[2]

International Voter Turnout

Voter turnout is one of many social indicators on which the United States ranks near the bottom among the world's developed democracies. In recent national elections (table 4.1), the U.S. turnout ranked second-to-last only to Switzerland among nations belonging to the Organisation for Economic Co-operation and Development (OECD). U.S. turnout fares poorly even in comparison to the turnout in many nondemocratic nations. Among the 140 countries holding two or more elections between 1948 and 1998, U.S. voter turnout ranked 114.[3]

For some, the embarrassing low American voter turnout reflects systemic flaws in American culture. Robert Putnam argues that low and declining voter turnout is the "canary in the mining pit," and indicative of a general lack of civic engagement.[4] Often low turnout is linked to pervasive American individualism and public distrust of government. Others argue that Americans have been alienated and turned off by politics and blame nasty election campaigning, talk radio, and divisively partisan incumbent politicians. Still others argue that low voter turnout is a consequence of an undemocratic electoral and political system that goes out of its way to make voting, particularly poor-and-minority voting, more difficult.[5]

Other scholars have challenged this "myth of the disengaged American voter."[6] First consider that Americans actually vote much more often than the citizens of other democracies; no other democracy offers its citizens as many opportunities to vote. The United States holds congressional elections every two years, about twice as often as most parliamentary democracies. Many states also conduct statewide elections during odd-numbered years and some schedule local elections separately from statewide elections. Almost all of these elections involve both a primary and general election. Few countries hold primary elections and rarer still is the practice of several American states of holding "open" primaries, permitting nonmembers of political parties to participate. Moreover, the number of offices Americans vote for is truly ex-

TABLE 4.1
Voter Turnout in Recent Parliamentary Elections: OECD Nations
(% of the voting age population)

	National Registry?	Year	Turnout	Year	Turnout	Average
Australia* (cv)		1996	82.5	1998	81.8	82
Austria	yes	1995	78.6	1999	72.6	76
Belgium (cv)	yes	1995	83.2	1999	83.2	83
Canada*		1997	56.2	2000	54.6	55
Denmark	yes	1994	81.7	1998	83.1	82
Finland	yes	1995	71.1	1999	65.2	68
France*		1993	61.3	1997	59.9	61
Germany		1994	72.4	1998	75.3	74
Greece		1996	83.9	2000	89.0	86
Hungary		1994	69.4	1998	59.0	64
Iceland	yes	1995	87.8	1999	86.2	87
Ireland	yes	1992	73.7	1997	66.7	70
Italy		1996	87.4	2001	84.9	86
Japan		1996	59.8	2000	59.0	59
Korea		1996	65.3	2000	55.7	61
Luxembourg (cv)**	yes	1994	60.5	1999	56.9	59
Mexico		1997	54.4	2000	59.7	57
Netherlands	yes	1994	75.2	1998	70.1	73
New Zealand		1996	83.0	1999	74.6	79
Norway	yes	1997	76.9	2001	73.0	75
Poland		1997	48.8	2001	47.6	48
Portugal		1995	79.1	1999	69.3	74
Slovak Republic	yes	1994	75.9	1998	78.9	77
Spain	yes	1996	80.6	2000	73.8	77
Sweden	yes	1994	83.6	1998	77.7	81
Switzerland	yes	1995	35.7	1999	34.9	35
Turkey		1995	79.1	1999	80.4	80
United Kingdom*		1997	69.4	2001	57.6	64
United States*		1996	49.1	2000	46.6	48

*Single-member district election (not proportional).
**(cv) strict enforcement of compulsory voting.
Sources: International Institute for Democracy and Electoral Assistance (http://www.idea.int); ACE Electoral
    Knowledge Network, http://aceproject.org/epic-en/vr/Epic_view/VR05.

ceptional. Illinois, for example, holds elections for county legislators, judges, treasurers, clerks, recorders, assessors, and coroners. Within each county overlapping city, township, and school districts also have elective assemblies, boards, and executive offices. In addition, many states regularly offer voters a bewildering array of ballot referenda.

We should also consider that voting is not the only means of citizen participation. The Comparative Study of Electoral Systems (CSES) project provides

"Over the past five years or so, have you done any of the
following things to express your views about something the
government should or should not be doing? ...

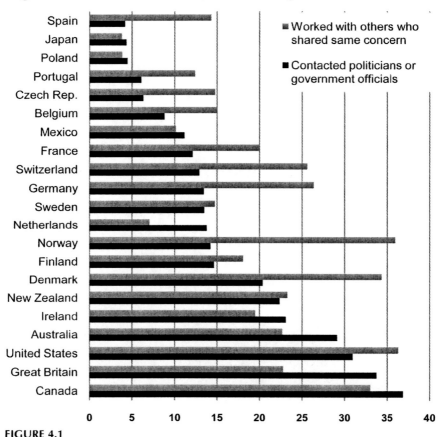

FIGURE 4.1
Cross-National Measures of Civic Participation
Source: The Comparative Study of Electoral Systems (www.cses.org). CSES Module 2 Fourth Advance Release. April 10, 2006.

data obtained from a common module of questions asked in surveys conducted just after the national elections held in most OECD, and several other, nations. Russell Dalton cites these data to argue that Americans, on a wide variety of CSES measures of civic and electoral participation, consistently surpass the citizens of most other nations.[7] In figure 4.1 we see that, when asked if they have contacted government officials or worked with others on a political issue, Americans ranked among the most engaged in political affairs. In-

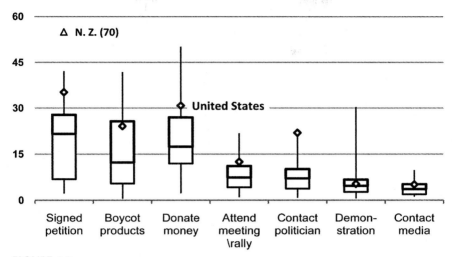

FIGURE 4.2
Participation in Political Activities in the Past Year, 2004
Source: International Social Survey Programme, 39 Nation Citizenship Survey, 2004, http://www.issp.org/.

terestingly, the six English-speaking countries have the highest rates of people contacting government officials.

A separate set of national surveys conducted in 2004 by the International Social Survey Programme asked respondents whether they had participated in each of seven political activities over the previous year. Of the thirty-nine nations surveyed, the United States scored in the top quartile on most of the items and above average on all seven (figure 4.2).

If American political culture does not account for the low voter turnout, the more likely explanations would have to do with some of the peculiar aspects of American electoral systems. Of the OECD nations shown in table 4.1, only five: Great Britain, France, Australia, Canada, and the United States, use single-member legislative districts for national legislative elections. The others use some form of proportional representation, a system that provides minor parties a better chance at gaining legislative seats. Of the five single-member district countries, only Australia has a record of high voter turnout, perhaps because it is one of only three countries that strictly enforces a compulsory voting law. Single-member districts are less likely to have close elections, and generally offer voters less reason to come to the polls. This is exacerbated in the United States (and not the other four) by political gerrymandering—the process by which elected officials choose their voters rather than the other way around. Although the past two presidential elections have been very close contests, the American Electoral College works to leave most states largely uncontested.

The U.S. system of voter registration, with most states requiring that voters register at least thirty days before the election, is also a significant impediment to voting. Many European and Latin American countries have what is in effect an automatic system of voter registration using some form of universal "national registry."[8] As shown in table 4.1, these countries generally have higher voter turnout than those using a two-stage, register-then-vote process. Moreover, few countries other than the United States hold elections on workdays rather than on a Sunday or national holiday. The one unique feature of the American election system that one would expect to result in higher voter turnout—the enormous sums of money spent on election campaign advertisement—does not seem to help.

Measuring U.S. Voter Turnout

One would think that calculating a statistic like voter turnout would be straightforward. The statistic is simple enough: the percentage of people who voted. When it comes to actually constructing the indicator, however, we find that there are consequential choices to be made in defining both the numerator and the denominator.

With the international data shown in table 4.1, and the most commonly cited U.S. turnout measure, the numerator count is not the number of people who "turned out" to vote, but the number of valid votes cast for the highest office on the ballot. This is done partly because many countries, and some states, only count the number of people who show up at the polls and cast valid votes. Some voters, however, may not vote for the highest office, and for other reasons, as Americans learned in the 2000 election, the number of valid votes cast can be less than the number of votes people intended to cast.

Most commonly, the voting age population is used as the divisor: in the 2004 U.S. election 125 million votes were cast for president, 58.3 percent of the 216 million people of voting age (see the "VC/VAP" series in figure 4.3). Although by this measure the 2004 turnout represented a significant improvement over 2000 (it was the second consecutive very close presidential election), the general trend in U.S. voter turnout since World War II has been down.

Although there are some uncounted votes, the "votes cast" turnout statistics, based on actual election records, can represent a reliable measure of voter turnout for the population as a whole, but the data are often not of much use to researchers who wish to investigate who voted and why. Because the voting is by secret ballot, the votes-cast data cannot tell us whether women, blacks, evangelical Protestants, conservatives, or any other group other than those de-

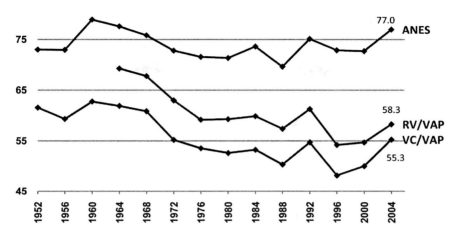

VC - votes cast   RV - reported votinng   VAP - voting age population
ANES: American National Election Survey

FIGURE 4.3
Three Measures of Voter Turnout, 1952–2004
Sources: U.S. Elections Project , http://elections.gmu.edu. U.S. Census Bureau, Current Population Survey,
  http://census.gov/population/www/docdemo/voting.html.

fined by electoral boundaries, voted in high or low numbers. To analyze turnout among different parts of the electorate, we have to rely on surveys.

Two different surveys provide the evidence for most of the research of American voting behavior. The American National Election Studies (ANES) survey, conducted for presidential and congressional elections since 1948, is based on face-to-face, pre- and postelection interviews, usually, of over 1,400 respondents. The ANES survey has been the key data for most of the political science research on American voting behavior, but as we see in figure 4.3, the ANES dramatically and increasingly overestimates the percentage of Americans who vote. Although the survey has a sampling error of only about 3 percent, 77 percent of ANES respondents reported voting in 2004 while the votes-cast turnout was just over 55 percent.

There are many reasons for this discrepancy. One is a phenomenon known as the Hawthorne effect: because respondents know they are being studied, their behavior changes. The ANES interviews the same respondents both before and after the election and asks them whether they voted in the postelection survey. Thus, the preelection interview may taint the postelection turnout data: sitting through an hour-long preelection interview about political issues may make people more likely to vote. Second, although the ANES is much more rigorous than most election polls in its efforts to contact respondents, the survey suffers from an increasing nonresponse rate.[9] The discrepancy between votes-cast turnout numbers and the ANES turnout numbers has increased over the years as the response rate to the postelection survey has dropped from the mid-70 percent range to the low-50 percent range. It is reasonable to speculate that those least likely to participate in election surveys are also least likely to vote.

The ANES survey may also suffer from a phenomenon known as a sample-mortality effect. Having sat through the preelection survey, those respondents least interested in politics and least likely to vote may have been most unwilling to participate in the second interview.

The final reason for the high ANES turnout rates is the most discouraging of all: people lie. It's not that they forget; the postelection interviews are conducted in the month right after the election. We know they lie and we even know who the liars are because the ANES cross-checks the respondents' answers with their actual voting records. Since 1972, the ANES validated-voter data has consistently indicated that over 40 percent of the people who had not actually voted said that they had. Southern whites, African Americans, Latinos, college-educated persons, and (this is most discouraging) frequent churchgoers are among those most likely to "overreport" voting.[10] The dirty little secret of voting behavior research is that this is the only question that has been cross-checked: we do not know how many people lied in response to the other questions that the interviewers asked. Separate analyses have shown that the rates of church attendance reported in major national surveys are about twice that of actual church attendance, suggesting that the relationship between church going and voting may have something to do with the same people lying on both questions.[11] It should be a bumper sticker: statistics don't lie, people do!

The U.S. Census Bureau conducts the second commonly used voting behavior survey, the November Current Population Survey following each congressional election. The Census "reported voting" turnout estimates, although higher than the votes-cast estimates, are generally more reliable than the ANES figures. In recent elections, the Census turnout data is based on phone and face-to-face interviews with over 60,000 adults; the November 2000 survey had a response rate of 87 percent compared to the ANES's 52 percent.[12] The Census survey allows for demographic analyses of voter turnout, but it lacks party affiliation and political attitudinal questions that inform much of voting behavior research done with ANES data. While the ANES turnout rate increasingly diverges from the actual votes-cast rate, the Census estimate is getting closer. The Census reported-voting turnout rate (RV\VAP in figure 4.3) for the 2004 election was 58.3 percent, only three percentage points higher than the votes-cast rate.[13] Perhaps Americans are becoming less likely to lie to their government. If only it were the other way around.

Using the Census reported-voting turnout numbers, we see that the general decline in voter turnout has occurred primarily among the youngest voters

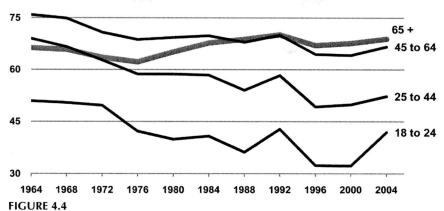

FIGURE 4.4
Reported Voter Turnout by Age
Source: U.S. Census Bureau, Current Population Survey.

(figure 4.4). Those over age 65 have actually increased their voting rates and, because the size of the elderly population is increasing faster than the rest of the population, their voting power has increased dramatically. Nevertheless, in the 2004 election the pattern may have reversed itself as the youngest voters showed a greater increase in turnout.

Education has a strong positive correlation with voter turnout (figure 4.5), even though the elderly, who have the highest turnout rates, generally have lower levels of educational attainment. Although the United States' sorry history of denying African Americans the vote underlies much of the conflict over voting rights, black voter turnout is only marginally less than that of whites,

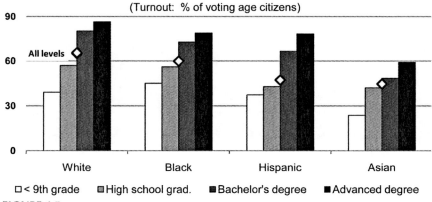

FIGURE 4.5
Reported Voter Turnout by Education and Race, 2004
Source: U.S. Census Bureau, Current Population Survey.

particularly when we considered differences in education. White turnout was 65 percent in the 2004 election compared to 60 percent for blacks, but among the least educated, blacks are actually more likely to vote. Racial differences in age and life expectancy also account for some of the black–white voting difference. Asian and Hispanic voter turnout, however, is dramatically lower even when "voting age citizens" is used as the turnout rate denominator.

Political commentary about turned-off voters reached its peak after the 1996 election when the votes-cast measure of voter turnout fell below 50 percent. In 2001, however, political scientist Michael McDonald compiled new data suggesting that the talk about the vanishing American voter was "a myth."[14] McDonald's analysis called attention to the denominator in the voting turnout statistic: *voting age population,* and argued that we should instead use the *voting eligible population.* Over recent elections, an increasing percentage of the American voting age population has not been eligible to vote. Mostly this is because of increasing immigration: both legal and nonlegal noncitizen residents are counted in the Census Bureau voting age population figures. In addition, in all but two states, prisoners are not allowed to vote and in twelve states even ex-felons are disenfranchised. Because the percentage of the American population that either is incarcerated or has ex-felon status has risen dramatically since the 1980s, an increasing percentage of the voting age population cannot vote. The Sentencing Project estimates that felony disenfranchisement laws have the effect of disenfranchising 13 percent of all black males.[15] Taking the votes cast as a percentage of the voting eligible population

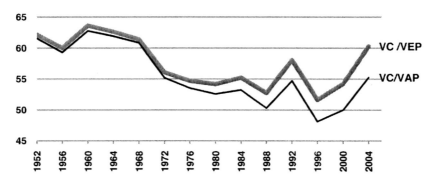

VC - votes cast VAP - voting age population
VEP - voting eligible population

FIGURE 4.6
Turnout: Percentage of Voting Age and Voting Eligible Populations
Sources: U.S. Elections Project : http://elections.gmu.edu; U.S. Census Bureau, http://census.gov/
population/www/docdemo/voting.html.

(the "VC/VEP" trend in figure 4.6) as our measure of turnout, we see no general decline in voter turnout since 1972, when eighteen-year-olds were given the franchise. In 2004, over 60 percent of voter-eligible Americans voted, the highest turnout rate since the 1968 election.

So which is the better measure of voter turnout? It depends on just what you are trying to measure. For McDonald, voter turnout is a measure of civic engagement. McDonald's use of the voting eligible population is appropriate when he is addressing arguments having to do with how well the election process inspires potential voters to participate in the elections. However, if you look at the voter turnout as a measure of how democratic a society is, the traditional "votes cast as a percentage of voting age population" numbers have greater validity. Although voting eligible turnout is increasing and at a long-time high, this is true in part due to the degree that the nation has become less democratic. It is because so many young black males (unlikely voters to begin with) have been put in jail and, in many states, denied the right to vote for the rest of their lives and because so many of our nation's poor are not citizens that voter turnout is as high as it is. If all young voters (the age group least likely to vote) were incarcerated and all the poor (the economic group least likely to vote) were declared noncitizens, the American voter turnout rate would be among the highest in the world, but the United States would not be a more democratic society.

Analyzing a Relationship: Election Day Registration

A common explanation for low American voter turnout is that American election rules generally create significant barriers to voting. Democratic partisans often allege that these barriers are intentional and designed to make it more difficult for new voters and poor voters to participate in elections. Defenders of these election rules argue that they are designed to preserve the integrity of elections and to discourage voter fraud.

One of the alleged barriers to voter participation is the requirement of most states that voters register for elections, usually one month before Election Day. Six American states allow voters to register on Election Day, when they show up to vote. Many credit Jesse Ventura's election as governor of Minnesota in 1998 to the state's Election Day registration (EDR) procedure. In the closing weeks of the campaign, Ventura's Reform Party campaign caught fire, attracting new and younger voters to the polls, many of whom might not have been able to vote had standard registration policies been in effect.

One of the groups advocating Election Day registration is Demos, a nonpartisan public policy research and advocacy organization. To support its position, Demos distributes a four-page advocacy toolkit that features, on its cover, a large bar chart indicating that in the 2004 election the six states (Idaho, Maine, Minnesota, New Hampshire, Wisconsin, and Wyoming) with Election Day registration recorded a 75.1 percent voter turnout, compared to 63.2 percent in the remaining states.[16] In the 2000 election, turnout in these EDR states was 68.2 percent, compared to 59.2 percent in the other states. Demos summarizes the data:

> EDR significantly increases the opportunity to cast a vote and participate in American democracy. Six states—Idaho, Maine, Minnesota, New Hampshire, Wisconsin, and Wyoming—offered EDR in the 2004 presidential election. These states boasted, on average, voter turnout that was 12 percentage points higher than in non-EDR states, and reported few problems with fraud, costs, or administrative complexity.[17]

Here, Demos states a descriptive conclusion (EDR states have higher turnout), but they clearly imply a causal explanation: Election Day registration causes a higher voter turnout. To assess whether this is a reasonable assumption, we must first examine the reliability and validity of the data. One possible source of unreliability has to do with the measure of voter turnout used. The Demos data are the Census's "reported" voter turnout numbers. Nevertheless, it is unlikely that this measurement affects the basic relationship. Reported voting turnout differed only marginally from votes-cast turnout in 2004 and there is no reason to assume that the residents of the EDR states are any less honest than those of the non-EDR states. In fact, citizens of Minnesota are famous for their honesty.

A second measurement problem has a more likely bearing on the relationship. The Demos data measure turnout as a percentage of the voting age population. In general, the six EDR states (five of them bordering Canada) do not have large immigrant populations, and they have generally lenient provisions for felon and ex-felon voting. EDR state of Maine is one of only two states (Vermont is the other) that allows prison inmates to vote. Of the twelve states that disenfranchise ex-felons, Wyoming (with a five-year waiting period) is the only EDR state. New Hampshire and Maine are among the twenty states that grant voting rights to those on probation and parole.

In Table 4.2, we see that the differences in turnout rates between EDR and non-EDR states are somewhat smaller when voting eligible population is used as the divisor. We can conclude that part, but not all, of the reason EDR states have higher turnout is that a higher percentage of their population is eligible to vote.

Next, we must consider the possibility that some other factors might account for the relatively higher voter turnout in EDR states. First, it is possible that the EDR states happened to have more contentious elections during these years. These states may have been targeted by the presidential election cam-

TABLE 4.2
Voter Turnout* in States with and without Election Day Registration, 1996–2004

	Votes Cast for President					
	Voting Age Population			*Voting Eligible Population*		
	1996	*2000*	*2004*	*1996*	*2000*	*2004*
EDR states	59.3	62.6	67.0	60.9	64.6	69.7
Non-EDR states	49.5	51.2	56.5	52.4	54.7	61.0
Difference	+9.8	+11.4	+10.4	+8.5	+9.9	+8.7

*Unweighted state averages.
Source: United States Elections Project, http://elections.gmu.edu/voter_turnout.htm.

paigns as close, or there may have been closely contested gubernatorial or Senate elections.

Also consider that the six EDR states are unlike the other states in many ways and some aspect of the political culture of these states may account for their higher voter turnout. One measure of a state's political culture is Robert Putnam's Social Capital Index.[18] The index combines thirteen measures[19] of civic engagement relating to participation in community organizations, public affairs, volunteerism, and attitudes of public trust and sociability. The scatterplot in figure 4.7, using the average turnout over three elections to partially discount the effect of particularly contentious elections, indicates that social capital is strongly related to both Election Day registration laws and voter

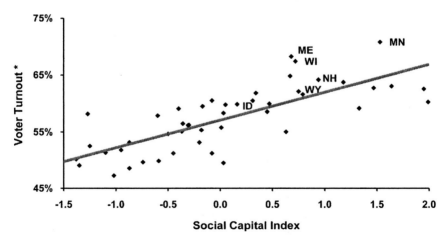

*Average votes cast / eligible population: 1996, 2000 and 2004
FIGURE 4.7
Social Capital and Average Voter Turnout, 1996–2004
Sources: United States Elections Project, http://elections.gmu.edu/; *Bowling Alone* website, http://www .bowlingalone.com/.

turnout. Nevertheless, all six EDR states have registered higher voter turnout than would be expected even after their social capital scores are taken into account.

Even so, social capital is not the only factor that may account for this relationship. A variety of factors peculiar to the six states or idiosyncratic factors peculiar to each of the states and the three elections may be at work here. One final strategy for evaluating the evidence is to consider time series analysis and a before-and-after comparison of the effects of changes in the laws as shown in table 4.3. Unfortunately three of the states (Maine, Minnesota, and Wisconsin, the three with the highest voter turnout) have had Election Day registration since at least the 1976 election, and the voter eligible turnout data only goes back to 1980. On the plus side, we can add Oregon, which permitted Election Day registration only in the 1980 and 1984 elections. This leaves us with four states (Oregon, Idaho, New Hampshire, and Maine) where we can compare voter turnout rates before and after a change in their registration laws.

Here the evidence proves most disappointing for advocates of Election Day registration. Compared to the turnout in states that have never used Election Day registration, Oregon's turnout changed little after Election Day registra-

TABLE 4.3
Voter Turnout* under Election Day Registration, 1980–2004

	1980	1984	1988	1992	1996	2000	2004
Maine	65	66	62	74	65	67	72
Minnesota	71	70	68	74	66	70	77
Wisconsin	68	65	63	70	58	68	76
Idaho	69	62	61	66	59	57	63
New Hampshire	58	54	56	66	58	64	70
Wyoming	54	56	56	62	61	59	64
Oregon	63	64	61	68	60	65	70
Never-EDR states	55	56	54	59	52	55	61
Difference from Never-EDR State Average							
Maine	10	10	9	15	13	13	11
Minnesota	16	14	14	15	14	15	16
Wisconsin	13	9	9	11	6	13	15
Idaho	14	6	7	7	7	3	2
New Hampshire	3	−2	3	7	6	9	9
Wyoming	−1	0	2	3	9	5	3
Oregon	8	8	7	9	7	10	9
Average difference	12	10	8	10	9	10	10

Shaded = election day registration.
*Turnout: Votes cast for president/voting eligible population.
Source: United States Elections Project, http://elections.gmu.edu/.

tion was discontinued. New Hampshire and Wyoming register improved turnout under the laws, but in Idaho, the turnout has been lower since the law went into effect.

Considering all of this evidence, what can we conclude about the effect of Election Day registration laws?

Based on the evidence presented here, there is no reason to believe that Election Day registration will result in dramatic voter turnout gains in normal presidential elections. But be aware of the limitations of the evidence. All the data shown here concerned presidential elections. If Election Day registration laws do affect turnout, one might expect that the most dramatic effects would be in nonpresidential elections that usually have lower turnout, such as Ventura's gubernatorial election. Evaluating the effect of the laws on off-year elections would require a far more elaborate analysis, taking into account the differences in the nature of each election campaign. Nor do we know what effect Election Day registration might have in presidential elections in states with historically low voter turnout. The states that have implemented these laws were high social capital and high turnout states to begin with. Except for the lack of evidence, there is every reason to believe that the laws would have their greatest impact in low social capital and low turnout states. However, the phrase "except for the lack of evidence" is a crucial qualification, and we may never know what would happen in the EDR states were Jesse Ventura to run for president.

Notes

1. George W. Bush, "President's Address to the Nation," The White House Office of the Press Secretary, December 18, 2005, at www.whitehouse.gov/news/releases/2005/12/20051218-2.html.

2. V. O. Key, Jr. *Southern Politics in State and Nation* (New York: Alfred A. Knopf, 1949).

3. International Institute for Democracy and Electoral Assistance, "Voter Turnout," March 7, 2005, at www.idea.int/vt/.

4. Robert D. Putnam, *Bowling Alone: The Collapse and Revival of American Community* (New York: Simon and Schuster, 2000), 35.

5. Frances Fox Piven and Richard A. Cloward, *Why Americans Still Don't Vote: And Why Politicians Want It That Way* (Boston, Mass.: Beacon Press, 2000).

6. Russell J. Dalton, "The Myth of the Disengaged American," *Public Opinion Pros,* October 2005, at www.publicopinionpros.com/features/2005/oct/dalton.asp.

7. Dalton, "The Myth of the Disengaged American."

8. R. Michael Alvarez, "Voter Registration," Caltech/MIT Voting Technology Project, April 30, 2001, at www.vote.caltech.edu/media/documents/testimony/050301_Alvarez.pdf.

9. For a debate on the role of response rate see Barry C. Burden, "Voter Turnout and the National Election Studies," *Political Analysis* 8 (July 2000): 389–98 and Michael

P. McDonald, "On the Overreport Bias of the National Election Study Turnout Rate," *Political Analysis* 11 (Spring 2003): 180–86.

10. Robert Bernstein, Anita Chadha, and Robert Montjoy, "Overreporting Voting: Why It Happens and Why It Matters," *Public Opinion Quarterly* 65 (Spring 2001): 22–44.

11. C. Kirk Hadaway, Penny Long Marler, and Mark Chaves, "What the Polls Don't Show: A Closer Look at U.S. Church Attendance," *American Sociological Review* 58(6): 741–52.

12. Benjamin Highton, "Self-Reported versus Proxy-Reported Voter Turnout in the Current Population Survey," *Public Opinion Quarterly* 69 (Spring 2005): 113–23.

13. Part of the difference between the "reported-voting" and "votes-cast" rates may be due to survey respondents who did not cast valid votes for president and to slightly different definitions of the voting age population.

14. Michael P. McDonald and Samuel Popkin, "The Myth of the Vanishing Voter," *American Political Science Review* 95, no. 4 (2001): 963–74.

15. The Sentencing Project, "Federal Voting Rights for People with Convictions," February 2007, at www.sentencingproject.org/Admin/Documents/publications/fd_bs_peoplewithconvictions.pdf.

16. Note that the average state turnout rates are higher than the turnout rate for the United States as a whole. This is because these are unweighted state averages. Small states usually have higher turnout than large states, and they disproportionately affect the state averages.

17. Demos, "Election Day Registration Helps America Vote," Summer-Fall 2006, at www.demos.org/pubs/EDR%20Toolkit%20070506.pdf.

18. Putnam, *Bowling Alone,* 288–95.

19. Putnam's Social Capital Index included voter turnout as one of fourteen variables in the index. Here, the index has been recalculated to exclude the turnout measure.

5

Measuring Educational Achievement

Weighing a hog doesn't make him fatter.—John Edwards, on the No Child Left Behind law

FOR THE MOST PART, I FIND TEACHING to be a most rewarding profession. If only I didn't have to grade those papers and exams. One would think that teachers would be pleased if someone were to offer to prepare and grade their students' exams for them. This has happened for our nation's public school teachers. Since 2005, state departments of education have developed, administered, and graded standardized tests in reading, writing, science, and mathematics annually for almost every student in grades three through eight and eleven. But many teachers and school officials are not happy, mostly because the tests are not used to grade the students so much as they are used to grade the schools, the school administrators, and the teachers. Just as students receive their grades on their report cards, states now send school district report cards to parents, reporting each school's and school district's scores on the tests. As a result, many teachers and administrators who have spent years listening to their students' excuses for poor test performance with bemused incredulity are now developing explanations of their own.

Much of the current effort to develop national standards for measuring student performance grew out of a 1983 report, *A Nation at Risk*, prepared by the National Commission on Excellence in Education. The report's opening sentences were meant to elicit alarm reminiscent of the reaction to the Soviet Union's launch of Sputnik in 1957:

Our Nation is at risk. Our once unchallenged preeminence in commerce, in-
dustry, science, and technological innovation is being overtaken by competi-
tors throughout the world.[1]

Among the evidence cited in support of the commission's conclusions were
the findings of several international measures of student learning:

International comparisons of student achievement, completed a decade ago, reveal that on 19 academic tests American students were never first or second and,
in comparison with other industrialized nations, were last seven times.[2]

The findings went against the conventional wisdom. The American economy
was the strongest in the world in large part due to advances in science and
technology. America had responded to the Sputnik challenge by landing a
man on the moon. In medicine, computers, communications, and industrial
technology, the United States was the unchallenged world leader. The number
of patents issued and Nobel prizes won far surpassed the rest of the world. The
reasons for the success, it was believed, were deeply embedded in American
culture and politics. While other nations' governments pursued socialist and
welfare state social policies, the United States promoted equality of opportunity by investing in education. The United States (and Germany) had led the
world in developing a universal public education system. American higher education enrollment topped the rest of the world and the prestige of U.S. colleges and universities was unquestioned.

International Education Indicators

Of the nineteen measures referred to in the *Nation at Risk* report, the most
comprehensive and reliable data were obtained from cross-national tests developed by the International Education Association (IEA): the First International Mathematics Study, conducted in the 1960s, and the First International
Science Study, conducted in the late 1960s and early 1970s. The results, shown
in table 5.1, were not good: the United States ranked near the bottom on most
tests, especially those in the higher grades.

In subsequent years, other international tests were developed, standards for
the consistent administration of the tests were refined, and more countries
participated in the testing. Whether it was due to changes in the administration of the tests or an improvement in students learning, American students
did do somewhat better. Out of forty-five countries participating in the IEA's
2003 Trends in International Mathematics and Science Study (TIMSS), American students ranked 15th in math and 9th in science.[3] Some of the relative

TABLE 5.1
First International Mathematics and
Science Achievement Test Scores

	Participating Educational Systems	U.S. Rank
Mathematics		
Age 13	12	11
High school seniors:		
math students	12	12
nonmath	10	10
Science		
Age 10	12	4
Age 14	14	7
High school seniors	14	14

Source: Elliott A. Medrich and Jeanne Griffith, *International Mathematics and Science Assessment*, Report No. CNES 92-011 (Washington, D.C.: U.S. Department of Education, Office of Educational Research and Improvement, 1992).

improvement in the U.S. score, however, had to do with the large number of developing countries included in the 2003 study.

The Organisation for Economic Co-operation and Development (OECD) has sponsored a second international testing regimen, the Programme for International Student Assessment (PISA), conducted on three-year intervals since 2000, with fifty-seven countries participating in the 2006 study. The PISA tests have some advantages over the TIMSS. PISA includes tests in reading and problem solving in addition to math and science; the tests are said to emphasize "important knowledge and skills needed in adult life"; it targets students by age (fifteen-year-olds) rather than grade level, and it offers a more consistent comparison group when the analysis is limited to just the thirty OECD member countries.[4] Again, the United States has fared poorly. Of the six OECD countries that did worse on the tests than the United States, five were among the poorest OECD nations (table 5.2).

Reliability of International Education Measures

Although these are the best data available, many factors affect the reliability of the cross-national measures of educational achievement. The exams have to be translated into each country's native language and the comparability of test items, especially those involving more than simple mathematical expressions, may be affected by differences in language and vocabulary. The American students scored slightly above average on the 2003 PISA reading test, but designing comparable reading tests in different languages is an uncertain science. In math and science, differences in curriculum (at a given

TABLE 5.2
PISA Educational Achievement Indicators, 2003
(15-year-old students, 30 OECD Nations)

	Math	Reading	Science	Problem Solving	Average
Finland	544	543	548	548	546
Korea	542	534	538	550	541
Japan	534	498	548	547	532
Canada	532	528	519	529	527
Australia	524	525	525	530	526
New Zealand	523	522	521	533	525
Netherlands	538	513	524	520	524
Belgium	529	507	509	525	518
Switzerland	527	499	513	521	515
Czech Republic	516	489	523	516	511
Sweden	509	514	506	509	510
France	511	496	511	519	509
Ireland	503	515	505	498	506
Germany	503	491	502	513	503
Iceland	515	492	495	505	502
Denmark	514	492	475	517	500
OECD Average	**500**	**494**	**500**	**500**	**498**
Austria	506	491	491	506	498
Hungary	490	482	503	501	494
Poland	490	497	498	487	493
Norway	495	500	484	490	492
Slovak Republic	498	469	495	492	488
Luxembourg	493	479	483	494	487
United States	**483**	**495**	**491**	**477**	**487**
Spain	485	481	487	482	484
Italy	466	476	486	469	474
Portugal	466	478	468	470	470
Greece	445	472	481	448	462
Turkey	423	441	434	408	427
Mexico	385	400	405	384	394

Source: OECD Programme for International Student Assessment, PISA 2003 Country Profiles, http://pisacountry.acer.edu.au/.

grade level some students may be studying geometry biology in one country, algebra or physics in another) or the time of the school year the tests are administered may also affect results. The United States has been a leader among the world's nations in mainstreaming students with learning disabilities in regular schools; in other countries, many students with disabilities are schooled separately and may or may not be included in the national testing.

Most problematic are situations where positive features of the school system lead to misleadingly negative test score results. When the First International

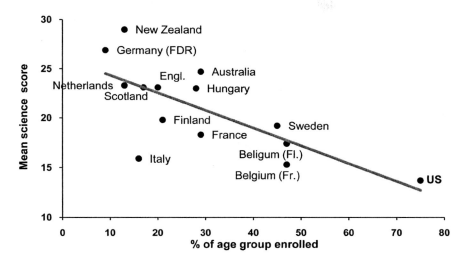

FIGURE 5.1
Enrollment and First International Science Study Results: Last Year of Secondary School
Source: Medrich and Griffith, International Mathematics and Science Assessment, table A.8, B.

Science tests were administered to high school seniors in 1969, the United States led the world in terms of the percentage of senior-year age cohort that was still enrolled in school, in part because many states required attendance up to age eighteen. Other countries either had higher dropout rates or, as in the case of West Germany, tracked working-class students into technical and vocational schools where the tests were not administered. As we see in figure 5.1, the exceptionally high rates of school enrollment in the United States account for the poor performance of high school seniors on the science test.

A good understanding of just who is and who is not being tested is crucial to any analysis of educational statistics. In the case of most international tests, the sampling begins with nationwide random samples of schools and the tests are given to either all students or a sample of students in attendance in the selected schools. In the case of the PISA tests, the sample of schools includes those schools that customarily enroll fifteen-year-olds (perhaps excluding American fifteen-year-olds held back in eighth grade) and then a sample of fifteen-year-olds within those schools.

Unlike the educational systems of almost every other country in the world that are run by centralized national or provincial education bureaucracies, American education is highly localized. Some argue that this accounts for the relatively poor performance of American students on international tests as the United States has lagged in the development of national curricular standards and tests to measure student performance. Local control has meant that the administration of nationwide tests in the United States often depends on the voluntary participation on the part of local school authorities. In other countries, a single national education bureaucracy can require that schools administer the international tests and assure uniform administration of the tests; in the United States, this requires the consent of local school boards or school principals. As a result, the United States typically had the lowest rates of participation in the tests. In the First International Science Study, only 43 percent of the sampled American schools agreed to participate while Australia, Hungary, Finland, and New Zealand had participation rates exceeding 98 percent.[5] In the 2003 PISA study, 82 of the 220 U.S. schools sampled refused to participate.[6]

One should always be suspicious of the effect of low response rates on education test scores: if the choice of participating in a study is given to school principals, one should expect that the principals who are most confident of their students' abilities may be most likely to agree to participate. Alternatively, participation may be highest in school districts where the school district bureaucracy exercises the most authority over the school principals. Low student response rates should also be suspected of contributing to artificially high scores. The best students are least likely to be absent on the day the tests are given. Especially when the tests are used to evaluate the performance of teachers and administrators, there may be ways of assuring that the weakest students are more likely to be absent, suspended, or in detention on the days the tests are given.

Analyzing International Education Data

In addition to being used for cross-national comparisons of education system performance, the international tests are used in research assessing the relationships between student achievement and cross-national and within-nation differences in school resources, curricula, approaches to teaching, family background, and home environment. For this purpose, the international studies also collect data on student demographics, student attitudes toward schooling, school resources, and school curriculum. One discovery of the early mathematics studies was that other countries were successfully teaching advanced mathematical concepts at an earlier age than American educators thought possible.[7]

A general finding of much of the research on educational achievement is that school resources, measured by factors such as the amount of money spent per pupil, teacher salaries, and class size do not have much effect on what students learn. The first and second IEA Mathematics and Science studies discovered that the countries with the largest class sizes (often, Asian countries) had the highest

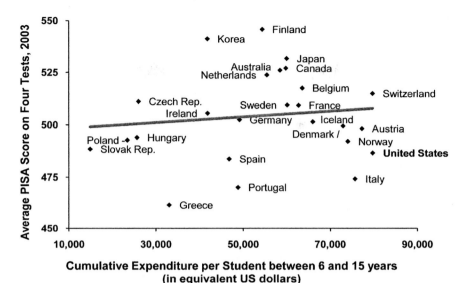

FIGURE 5.2
School Spending and Student Achievement: 25 OECD Nations
Source: OECD/PISA database, http://pisaweb.acer.edu.au/oecd_2003/oecd_pisa_data.html.

achievement scores. As we see in the case of the PISA tests (figure 5.2), there is little correlation between school spending and achievement, and lack of money certainly does not account for the poor U.S. performance on the tests.

The same studies that show that school resources have little effect on educational achievement also report that family resources have a strong influence. The consistent finding of educational research that students' family background, measured by the parents' occupational status, income, wealth, and level of education are the strongest determinants of educational achievement represents a critical constraint on all the world's education systems. Thus, we see in figure 5.3 that countries with the highest levels of student achievement tend to be those with adult populations that are more highly educated.

One of the most interesting cross-national studies of educational achievement was a small three-country study, conducted by Shin-ying Lee, Veronica Ichikawa, and Harold Stevenson in 1987.[8] Their findings suggested that parental attitudes accounted for the higher levels of math achievement of Japanese and Taiwanese students in comparison to American students (see figure 5.4). When asked why some students do better in math than others, the American mothers tended to say that some students are innately better at math than others. The Japanese and Taiwanese mothers insisted it was because some students work harder than others.

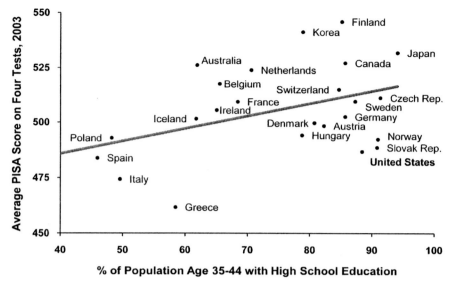

FIGURE 5.3
Educational Attainment and Student Achievement: 25 OECD Nations
Source: OECD/PISA database.

The general American belief that learning is a result of intellectual ability rather than hard work—an idea often expressed by students in my statistics courses—is a product, I think, of the American educational system's long infatuation with tests of intellectual ability, such as IQ tests and the SAT.

The Validity of Standardized Tests

For the most part, standardized educational tests are a mixture of aptitude tests and achievement tests. Aptitude tests are designed to measure intellectual ability separate from what students learn in the classroom. IQ tests are the purest form of an aptitude test: no matter what you have learned from your teachers, your IQ score changes very little from first grade to your senior year of college. The more closely a standardized test measures the mastery of a specific curriculum and subject matter, the more it measures achievement.

The SAT illustrates the subtle distinction between an aptitude test and an achievement test. When the test was first created in 1901, "SAT" stood for the Scholastic Achievement Test, but in 1941, the name was changed to the Scholastic Aptitude Test. In 1990, the SAT was renamed the Scholastic Assessment Test, with no clear indication of just what it was that the test was assess-

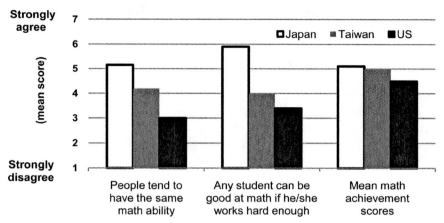

FIGURE 5.4
Mothers' Explanations for Math Achievement
Source: Lee, Ichikawa, and Stevenson, "Beliefs and Achievement," 157.

ing. Each of these changes reflected the intellectual fads and education politics of the time, matters that were settled once and for all in 1994 when the name was changed to just plain SAT. This, three years after Kentucky Fried Chicken became KFC, for much the same reason.

So what does the SAT measure and is it a valid measure of whatever it is that it measures? There has been extensive debate and research concerning the validity and reliability of the use of the SAT as a measure of individual academic achievement and ability.[9] Are the tests culturally biased? Does instruction in test-taking skills improve students' scores? Are there other kinds of intelligence that the test does not measure? How well does the test predict students' academic success in college? Regardless of whether the SAT is a valid measure of individual intelligence or learning, its validity as an aggregate social indicator depends on how it is used. The average SAT score of a freshman class is a very good measure of how stringent a college's admissions standards are, and increasing freshman SAT scores are a reasonable indicator that a college is becoming more competitive. For a long time, trends in SAT scores, particularly the declining scores of the 1970s and 1980s, were cited as a general indicator of the quality of the nation's elementary and secondary education. For the most part such conclusions were not valid, as changes in the percentage of high school students taking the test were the primary reason for the decline. Whether improvement in group SAT scores indicates educational improvements, as was suggested by the Simpson's paradox example in chapter 1 (table 1.4), depends on whether you think the changing racial composition of test-takers is a valid excuse for the stagnating total scores.

Testing American Students

On July 1, 1966, the U.S. Office of Education released what came to be known as the Coleman Report, a national study of educational achievement, conducted by sociologist James S. Coleman, based on verbal and mathematics tests administered to 600,000 students and 60,000 teachers in 4,000 schools.[10] The Office chose the day before the 4th of July weekend in hopes that reporters would not pay too much attention to Coleman's findings.[11] The findings, carefully hidden in the summaries of the report distributed at the press conference, were that school resources (school spending, class size, teachers' salaries, and school facilities) had little effect on student achievement and that socioeconomic status of the students' families was the primary determinant of how well students did in school. Subsequent research has largely confirmed the main findings, and the Report was significant in that it led to new efforts to measure what American students were learning and to significant advances in the statistical analysis of standardized education test score data.

The Nation's Report Card

Since 1969, more systematic national testing of student learning has been conducted under the National Assessment of Education Progress (NAEP),

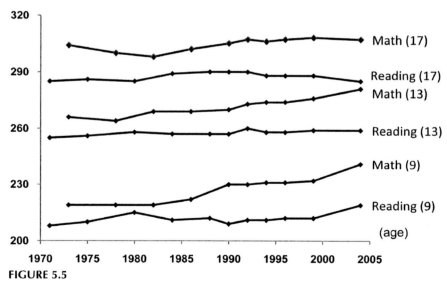

FIGURE 5.5
Trends in Average NAEP Reading and Math Scale Scores by Age, 1971–2004
Source: National Center for Education Statistics (NCES), The Condition of Education, 2007, table 15-1.

sometimes called the Nation's Report Card. The NAEP regularly tests a national sample of about 7,000 students in grades four, eight, and twelve (or ages 9, 13, and 17) in mathematics, science, reading, and writing, and in other subjects on an intermittent basis. In addition to the subject-matter testing, the NAEP also collects data on school and classroom characteristics, student demographics, and students' home environment. The NAEP sample is too small to provide scores for individual schools and only limited data for the fifty states are available, but it provides the best data for assessing national trends in student achievement and for evaluating general relationships between student achievement and other factors.

NAEP tests are scaled with a mean of about 150 at each grade level, but for the math, reading, and science tests the NAEP rescales the tests on a common "scale score" to allow for comparisons between different grade levels. Over time, there has been some improvement in student scale scores on the NAEP tests, particularly in elementary school math (figure 5.5). Scores have not gone up as fast at the high school level, but this may be due to fewer students dropping out of school before the test is administered.

The Racial Gap in Educational Achievement

The persistent racial and ethnic learning disparities are the most troubling finding of the American educational research. Using the scale score data in figure 5.6 we see the disparities between black and Hispanic students and whites

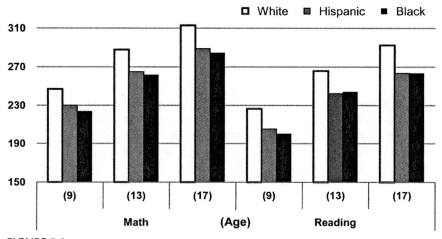

FIGURE 5.6
NAEP Math and History Scale Scores by Race, Ethnicity, and Age, 2001 and 2004
Source: NCES, NAEP Data Explorer, http://nces.ed.gov/nationsreportcard/nde/.

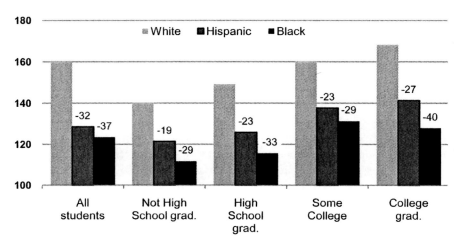

Parents' Education

FIGURE 5.7
NAEP Eighth Grade Science Scores by Race, Ethnicity, and Parents' Highest Level of Education, 2005
Source: NCES, NAEP Data Explorer.

in math and reading at ages 9, 13, and 17. In each subject area, seventeen-year-old black and Hispanic students score about the same as thirteen-year-old whites. Bluntly stated, African American and Latino students are graduating from high school with an eighth grade level of education.

The gaps narrow but do not disappear when one controls for measures of the students' family background. In the case of the NAEP science scores, shown in figure 5.7, the gap between Hispanic and white students' scores is reduced when comparing students with parents of the same level of education, but the black–white gap narrows less so.

As is illustrated with the reading scale scores in figure 5.8, there has been some improvement in the black–white learning gap in the elementary schools, but the scores for black high school students have not improved since the mid-1980s. The lack of improvement at the high school level, however, may be due to a substantial decline in the black high school dropout rate over this time.

The literature on the racial learning gap points to three possible explanations. Some authors, such as Jonathan Kozol, place the blame on racial disparities in school funding and racial segregation.[12] The United States has the most unequal system of school finance in the developed world and the levels of racial segregation in many of the nation's school systems surpasses the segregation at the time of the 1954 *Brown v. Board of Education* decision. More

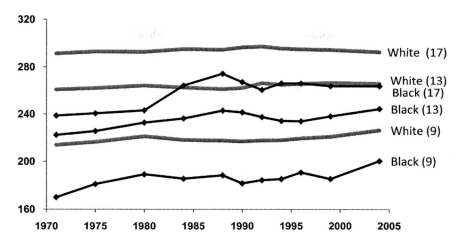

*non-Hispanic students (age)

FIGURE 5.8
Average NAEP Reading Scale Scores by Race* and Age
Source: NCES, Digest of Education Statistics, 2005, http://nces.ed.gov/programs/digest/d05/.

conservative scholars, such as Abigail Thernstrom and Stephan Thernstrom, point to culture and the home environment.[13] The racial disparities in learning, they argue, correlate strongly with racial differences in the prevalence of single-parent families, television viewing, and parental academic expectations. Still a third perspective, represented by Richard Rothstein, argues that the racial and ethnic disparities merely mask socioeconomic disparities in income, wealth, and parental education.[14]

Each of these perspectives is deeply involved in the controversy over a multitude of policy solutions designed to address the problem: school finance reform, bilingual education, multicultural education, school busing, preschool education, school vouchers, charter schools, smaller class size, smaller schools, longer school days, longer school years, same-sex schools, social promotion, training in parenting skills, and different approaches to school discipline and the teaching of reading and mathematics.

No Child Left Behind Testing

Under the No Child Left Behind (NCLB) law, signed by President George W. Bush on January 8, 2002, educational measurement has reached its zenith in the United States, at least in terms of the amount, if not the quality, of testing that is done. While the NAEP surveys a sample of only seven thousand students per subject at three grade levels, NCLB tests all students in grades three through eight and eleven in mathematics and reading. Science tests are administered to all students at three grade levels. Where the NAEP samples are too small to provide reliable data for individual schools and school districts, the explicit purpose of NCLB testing is to measure the schools' performance. Although, unlike the NAEP, the NCLB data have no sampling error, interpreting the test results is fraught with reliability and validity pitfalls.

NCLB requires each state to set "adequate yearly progress" (AYP) standards for its schools based on the percentage of students whose test scores meet a state-defined level of proficiency. The proficiency standard applies not only to the entire student body, but to each of several groups of students defined by race, ethnicity, low income ("school lunch eligible"), limited English proficiency, and learning disability (students with "individualized education plans").

Schools that fail to make AYP in one year (for any of the subgroups) and those that fail to improve in the second year are classified as "in need of improvement." The schools in need of improvement do not, as is often claimed, have their funding reduced: they actually become eligible for additional federal funds and students in the need-improvement schools may be given the opportunity to change schools or to receive tutorial assistance. Only if the schools fail for several years are they expected to implement more stringent policy changes, including reassigning or firing staff. In theory, the percentage of students who must be proficient to meet the AYP goals will increase each year until 2014, when all students will be expected to be proficient. This, and the fact that students classified as learning disabled or with limited English proficiency are expected to meet the same proficiency standard as other students, are among the more problematic aspects of the law.

Reliability and Validity of No Child Left Behind Data

Because the states design their own NCLB exams and set their own standards for what constitutes "proficiency," national AYP test results and cross-state comparisons of the test results, including the percentage of students who are proficient or the percentage of schools that meet AYP, are essentially meaningless. This is best demonstrated in a comparison of the percentage of students who meet state proficiency standards with the percentage who meet the national proficiency standard on the NAEP tests. Of the thirty-five states for which there are comparable NAEP data (shown in figure 5.9), all but three have a higher percentage of their students meeting the state eighth grade math standards than meet the national standard on the NAEP math tests.[15] The state pass rates do no correlate with the national standards at all. In most states more

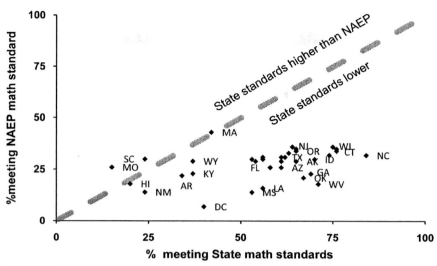

FIGURE 5.9
Percentage of Students Meeting State and National Eighth Grade Math Standards by State, 2005
Source: NCES, "Mapping 2005 State Proficiency Standards onto the NAEP Scales," June 2007.

than half the students meet the state standards, but in no state do more than half the students meet the national standard.

Within states, comparisons of year-to-year changes in NCLB test scores and measures of adequate yearly progress also pose problems of measurement reliability. Whereas the NAEP carefully maintains consistent measurement standards for the time series trend data it reports, state NCLB tests and standards often change. Because governors and state boards of education can be held publicly accountable for both the percentage of students who meet standards and the number of schools that make adequate progress, they have an incentive to make changes that make them look good. This can involve making improvements in the tests in ways that happen to improve scores, adjusting the weighting of components of the tests, or raising the minimum number of students needed for schools' subgroup population scores to be counted (the minimum subgroup size varies from fifteen to two hundred across the states).

Even in those states that do maintain a consistent testing regimen, several factors inherent in the testing threaten the validity of many conclusions drawn from trends in NCLB results. Because, by 2012, eighth grade students will have taken NCLB tests in each of their previous five years of schooling, some improvement in their scores should be expected due to a "testing effect": students learning how to take the exams more efficiently. On the other hand, there may be a reverse testing-effect at work. Students may become less motivated to do well on the tests as they learn that their scores on the tests do not affect their grades.

Improvements in scores may also reflect a "teaching to the test" phenomenon. As schools and teachers become more aware of the kinds of questions asked and the subject matter that is emphasized in the test, they may change what they emphasize in their teaching. To some extent, this is a good thing, as teachers adjust their teaching to state curricular standards. A similar problem may occur as schools and school districts focus their resources on the subjects that are tested and place less emphasis on subjects such as art, music, physical education, and history that are not tested.

Nevertheless, if the NCLB tests are well designed, they do provide reliable and generally valid measures of differences in student achievement across schools and school districts in the same state. This is to say that, on average, students in schools that score well on the math, reading, and science tests are indeed better at math, reading, and science than students in schools that score poorly. However, this does not mean that the schools' test scores are good measures of the quality of the education that the schools provide. American public schools tend to be highly segregated by race, ethnicity, and wealth, and these and related attributes of students' family background have much more to do with differences in school scores than what goes on in the classroom. To evaluate the quality of the education schools provide, these factors have to be taken into account.

The Worst Schools in the Nation

The Chicago public schools, once called the "worst in the nation" by Secretary of Education William Bennett, illustrate how misleading conclusions can be drawn from the raw NCLB data. Chicago public school students consistently do worse on the state tests, in each subject and at every grade level, than students in the state of Illinois as a whole. In 2006, just 62 percent of Chicago elementary schools students passed the state's NCLB tests, called the Illinois Standards Achievement Test (ISAT), compared to 77 percent statewide (including Chicago).

However, Chicago schools serve a student body that is substantially different from that of the rest of the state: 86 percent of Chicago public school students qualify for the school lunch program, compared to only 40 percent statewide and nearly 86 percent of the Chicago students are black or Hispanic, compared to less than 40 percent statewide. In 2006, over one hundred Chicago public elementary schools, nearly 20 percent of the district's schools,

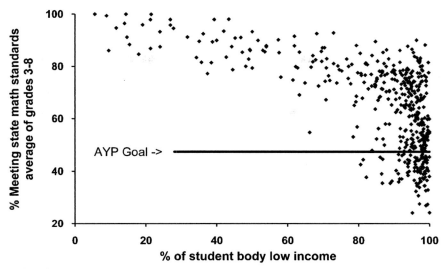

FIGURE 5.10
Low Income and Math Achievement in Chicago Public Schools, 2006
Source: Illinois State Board of Education, 2005–2006 Report Card Data, http://www.isbe.net/research/.

fell below the state goal of having 47.5 percent of the students scoring proficient on the math exams. In each school that failed to achieve the standard, more than 80 percent of the students were classified as low income, as determined by their eligibility for the school lunch program (see figure 5.10).

The Politician's Error

Nevertheless, the release of the 2006 ISAT scores was greeted with cheers. The *Chicago Tribune* announced the results in March 2007 with the headline: "Chicago Schools See Huge Gains on Test Score." The story reported that Chicago students' 62 percent pass rate on all the elementary grade tests was substantially higher than the 48 percent pass rate for 2005. The results were "extraordinarily encouraging," according to Chicago Public School system CEO, Arne Duncan, and district officials credited the gains to policy changes, including "after-school tutoring, better-trained teachers and new classroom assessments."[16]

The *Tribune* story did note that some might attribute the improvement to changes made to the tests.[17] The 2006 ISAT offered students more time to complete tests with fewer questions, an improved answer sheet, and color illustrations. The state lowered the passing score for the eighth grade math test to make it more in-line with the early grade scores. Subsequent stories reported other test changes that may have affected the results, such as giving less weight to the relatively difficult "response" items and more to multiple-choice questions.[18] There were good reasons for most of these changes, and they may have resulted in more valid tests, but the changes undermined the reliability of year-to-year comparisons.

Rufus Williams, president of the Chicago Board of Education, responded to critics who suggested that the changes in the test were the reason Chicago's students did so well:

> Our children can learn. They can achieve and they can compete. Their performance on the 2006 ISAT is but one measure of proof. To continually question their record-breaking results demonstrates an inability to believe that they can actually meet the high expectations that we must set for them. They are proving they can.[19]

This is an interesting counterargument, equivalent to Bush administration arguments that those who criticize his management of the Iraq War are actually criticizing the performance of the troops in the field. The next step in the argument is to claim that those who question the success of the administration's effort are actually encouraging its failure. But Williams cites hard evidence to support his claim: the Chicago students' gains were substantially higher than those of the students in the rest of Illinois: "Officials across the state agree that districts made gains all over Illinois, but Chicago Public Schools students led the way, gaining 14 percentage points on the test, compared to the overall state gain of 8 percentage points."[20]

Williams makes what might be a valid point: changes in the test may account for the statewide increase, but not the relative performance of the Chicago schools. Unfortunately, Williams's analysis involves a rate of change fallacy, involving comparisons of changes starting from different base numbers. It is true that the Chicago scores did improve from a 48 percent pass rate to 62 percent, while the Illinois scores improved from 69 percent to 77 percent (table 5.3). But look what happens if we recalculate the test results to show the percentage of students who failed. Chicago's failure rate went down 27 percent; Illinois' failure rate went down 26 percent. There is no meaningful difference between the two results.

The misinterpretation of educational statistics involving comparisons of changes from different numerical bases is so common that one educational researcher, Stephen Gorard, has given it a name: the "politician's error."[21] This is a little unfair to politicians, as even Gorard notes that the mistake frequently occurs in published educational research, particularly in research that concludes that groups of students who have not done well previously are "closing the gap."

TABLE 5.3
Chicago and Illinois ISAT Results, 2005–2006

	2005	2006	Net Change	% Change
Passing Rate				
Chicago Public Schools	48%	62%	+14	+29%
All Illinois Public Schools	69	77	+8	+12
Failure Rate				
Chicago Public Schools	62	48	−14	−27
All Illinois Public Schools	31	23	−8	−26

Source: Illinois State Board of Education, 2005-2006 Report Card Data.

Evidence That Chicago Schools Are Doing Well

So far the data suggest that Chicago students are less proficient than students in the rest of the state and that there is no reliable evidence that student performance improved either in Chicago or statewide in 2006. Nevertheless, a closer look at the city and state data suggest that there is some evidence that the Chicago public school system may be doing a better job of educating students than the school systems in the rest of the state.

The data in figure 5.11 tell the story. Let's begin with the reading pass rate for "all students" enrolled in the third grade. Just over half (51 percent) of Chicago third graders passed the reading test compared to 71 percent statewide. Nevertheless, when we look at the third grade scores more closely, breaking the data down by race, ethnicity, and income, we see that the 20 point city–state gap is substantially reduced. White Chicago third graders do almost as well as whites statewide and the gap for black, Hispanic, and low income students is only 7 percent or less. Thus we can conclude that for third graders, most of the 20 point city–state gap is due to differences in the racial, ethnic, and low income composition of the Chicago schools. Other factors may account for some of the gap that remains. Low income students in Chicago may be even poorer than the low income students statewide. Black, Hispanic and low income students in Chicago may be more likely to come from single-parent family homes than similar students statewide. Unfortunately, those data are not available and we do not know whether they would account for the gap that remains.

The strongest evidence in defense of the Chicago schools is seen when we examine the eighth grade math results, where the city–state gap for all students is 7 percent.[22] Pay no attention to the apparent Chicago improvement from third to eighth grade, the differences in the size of the gaps may merely be an artifact of differences in the two exams. More telling, however, is that for

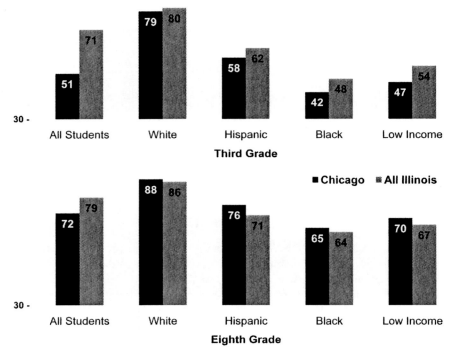

FIGURE 5.11
Percentage of Students Meeting State Math Standards: Chicago and Illinois, 2006
Source: Illinois State Board of Education, 2005–2006 Report Card Data.

white, Hispanic, black, and low income eighth grade students, Chicago schools scored higher than the rest of the state. Low income students, who were behind the state average in third grade, are three percentage points ahead in eighth grade.

It is difficult to imagine how anything other than better teaching in the Chicago schools might account for these results, but there are some alternative explanations. It is unlikely that there are any major differences in the family background of third and eighth grade students, in either Chicago or the rest of the state. There might be something peculiar about the eighth grade reading test, but other research shows the relative improvements in Chicago scores occur gradually over five grade levels from third to eighth.[23] One possible factor might be attendance. Chicago schools at all grade levels do have a slightly lower attendance rate than schools statewide, and it is likely that eighth grade attendance is worse than third grade attendance, but there are no data that would support or disprove this. Differences in school policies regarding social promotion—promoting students to the next grade regardless of their proficiency in the grade level subject matter—might explain the results. Chicago eliminated social promotion in 1996 and now requires that students pass a third, sixth, and eighth grade exam to be promoted to the next grade. Holding students back in grade results in older students at each grade level (a positive effect on test scores) especially in the upper grade levels, but it also results in weaker students taking the test twice (and this may have a negative effect). Unfortunately, there are no clear data for the rest of the Illinois school districts to examine the effect.

Searching for Excuses

Until the NCLB law was passed, there was very little systematic measurement of what students were actually learning in many of our nation's schools; but even with the law, cherry picked data and misleading interpretations of NCLB test results are commonplace. There is an understandable tendency for school officials to tout the initial aggregate results if they are positive, to look at other comparisons if they are not, and if those comparisons are not good, to search for other explanations that offer a positive spin on what is going on in the schools. Often this is more than justified, but the process is one-sided and leaves out the search for evidence that might explain away the positive results. This is unfortunate, because the law works best when school officials uncover disappointing results and make meaningful changes to address the problems.

When the 2006 eleventh grade Illinois high school test scores, released a week after the elementary tests, showed a slight decline in both the Illinois and Chicago ISAT results, state officials had an explanation: the eleventh graders did not have the benefit of the "standards-based" curriculum that had so dramatically improved the elementary students' performance. "Our kids in 11th grade didn't start their careers in standards-based classrooms," explained state assessment director, Becky McCabe, "Those 17-year-olds haven't had the same kind of instruction our elementary kids are getting now."[24]

Essentially the assessment director has found reasons to dismiss disappointing high school results, to embrace the seemingly positive elementary results, and to wait until the things that improved the elementary school scores begin to affect the high schools. No doubt, this will happen when the state discovers a reason for including more color graphics or lowering the passing grade on the high school tests.

If Chicago's schools have improved since the secretary of education called them the "worst in the nation," it is because they took the test score results that the secretary based his conclusion on seriously (Chicago had scored at the bottom among the nation's large-city school districts on a national test). The district instituted far-reaching reforms, including decentralizing the school district bureaucracy, holding principals accountable to elected school councils, and eliminating social promotion. None of this would have happened if they had found a way to explain away the results.

Notes

1. National Commission on Excellence in Education, *A Nation at Risk: The Imperative for Educational Reform*, April 1983, at www.ed.gov/pubs/NatAtRisk/index.html.

2. National Commission on Excellence in Education, *A Nation at Risk*.

3. National Center for Education Statistics, "Highlights from the Trends in International Mathematics and Science Study (TIMSS) 2003," tables 3 and 9 at nces.ed.gov/pubs2005/timss03/tables.asp.

4. Organisation for Economic Co-operation and Development, "OECD Programme for International Student Assessment," at www.pisa.oecd.org.

5. Elliott A. Medrich and Jeanne Griffith, *International Mathematics and Science Assessment: What Have We Learned?* Report no. CNES 92-011 (Washington, D.C.: U.S. Department of Education, Office of Educational Research and Improvement, 1992) at nces.ed.gov/pubs92/92011.pdf.

6. Elart von Collan, "OECD PISA—An Example of Stochastic Illiteracy?" *Economic Quality Control* 16, no. 2 (2001): 227–53, at www.heldermann-verlag.de/eqc/eqc01_16/eqc16016.pdf.

7. Medrich and Griffith, *International Mathematics*, 35.

8. Shin-ying Lee, Veronica Ichikawa, and Harold W. Stevenson, "Beliefs and Achievement in Mathematics and Reading: A Cross National Study of Chinese, Japanese and American Children and their Mothers," in *Advances in Motivation and Achievement*, vol. 7, Martin Maehr and Douglas A. Kleiber (Greenwich, Conn: JAI Press, 1987), 149–79.

9. Nicholas Lemann, *The Big Test: The Secret History of the American Meritocracy* (New York: Farrar, Straus and Giroux, 1999).

10. James S. Coleman, Ernest Q. Campbell, Carol J. Hobson, James McPartland, Alexander M. Mood, Frederic D. Weinfeld, and Robert L. York, *Equality of Educational Opportunity* (Washington, D.C.: U.S. Government Printing Office, 1966).

11. Gerald Grant "Shaping Social Policy: The Politics of the Coleman Report," *Teachers College Record* 75, no. 1 (September 1973): 17–54.

12. Jonathan Kozol, *The Shame of the Nation: The Restoration of Apartheid Schooling in America* (New York: Crown Publishers, 2005).

13. Stephan Thernstrom and Abigail Thernstrom, *No Excuses: Closing the Racial Gap in Learning* (New York: Simon and Schuster, 2003).

14. Richard Rothstein, *Class and Schools: Using Social, Economic and Educational Reform to Close the Black–White Achievement Gap* (Washington, D.C.: Economic Policy Institute, 2004).

15. National Center for Education Statistics, "Mapping 2005 State Proficiency Standards onto the NAEP Scales," June 2007, at nces.ed.gov/nationsreportcard/pubs/studies/2007482.asp.

16. Tracy Dell'Angela, "Chicago Schools See Huge Gains on Test Scores," *Chicago Tribune*, March 6, 2007, 1.

17. In 2004, a new contractor, Harcourt Assessment, was chosen to redesign the tests. This, just after Harcourt hired a former aide and political advisor to the governor as a lobbyist. See Naarah Patton, "Harcourt Contract: Saga a Fiasco," April 11, 2006, at www.susanohanian.org/atrocity_fetch.php?id=5862.

18. Diane Rado, "Scoring Method on ISAT Faulted: Big Gains Could Have Been Inflated, State Adviser Says," *Chicago Tribune*, April 13, 2007, 1.

19. Rufus Williams, "Students' Performance Has Amazed All," *Chicago Tribune*, March 21, 2007, Letters to the Editor.

20. Williams, "Students' Performance Has Amazed All."

21. Stephen Gorard, "Keeping a Sense of Proportion: The 'Politician's Error' in Analysing School Outcomes," *British Journal of Educational Studies*, 47, no. 3 (September 1999): 235–46.

22. One should not make too much of "all students" change from third to eighth grade as these are different tests and the smaller gap may be due to less variation in the eighth grade scores.

23. John Q. Easton, Stuart Luppescu, and Todd Rosenkranz, "2006 ISAT Reading and Math Scores in Chicago and the Rest of the State," Consortium on Chicago School Research at the University of Chicago, June 2007, at ccsr.uchicago.edu/content/publications.php?pub_id=115.

24. Rosalind Rossi, Art Golab, and Kate N. Grossman, "Tardy State High School Scores Show Few Gains: Science, Reading Down, but Math Results Up a Bit," *Chicago Sun-Times*, March 13, 2007, 16.

6

Measuring Poverty and Inequality

D O FREE MARKETS AND GLOBALIZATION foster greater or lesser poverty and inequality in the developing world? Does international development assistance to third world nations alleviate or exacerbate the conditions of poverty? Do welfare state social policies significantly reduce poverty in developed nations? What impact did the U.S. 1996 welfare reform act have on the nation's poor? Are the relatively high rates of poverty in the United States due to the dysfunctional behavior of the poor, to racism and discrimination, or to stingy social policies? How do these factors account for the feminization of poverty in the United States? Is it true what they say, "The rich are getting richer and the poor, poorer"?

The arguments, policy evaluations, political debates, and academic research concerning these questions rely on measurements of the incidence of poverty. Poverty rates generally measure the percentage of the population living in households whose annual income (or, as we shall see, annual expenditure) falls below a predetermined poverty threshold. There are two different approaches to defining what standard of living constitutes poverty. Absolute poverty thresholds define a level below which households lack basic necessary goods and services. Relative thresholds measure the percentage of the population living at a standard well below the average of their fellow citizens.

Neither strategy for defining poverty is ideal. Poverty is relative and absolute standards of measuring it are inherently arbitrary. Relative poverty thresholds measure inequality more than they measure a consistent level of deprivation. For these and other reasons, debates about poverty often end up being debates about the measurement of poverty. Liberal scholars[1] often argue that poverty rate statistics underestimate the true dimensions of poverty and that higher poverty thresholds should be used, while conservatives[2] insist that the statistics exaggerate poverty, either because the thresholds are set too low or because the measure of family income does not include all the resources available to the families who are classified as poor.

Measuring Poverty in Developing Nations

Since the early 1980s, two indicators developed by the World Bank have been the standard measures of poverty in low and middle income nations. The Bank defines "extreme poverty" as the percentage of a country's population living in households consuming less than $1 a day, in 1993 dollars. Wealthier, or middle income, countries use a $2 a day threshold as the more general poverty indicator.[3] Both thresholds are expressed in constant U.S. dollars and are adjusted for price differences in consumer goods between countries, using measures of national currencies' purchasing power parity (PPP). In a country with an average family size of four persons, the $1 a day standard would mean a family poverty threshold of $1,424 per year. In some countries, the poverty measures are based on the number of persons in families with incomes below the poverty threshold, but in the poorest nations (where subsistence agriculture and noncash economies predominate), the indicators use estimates of consumption—the value of the goods and services consumed by families.

In 2001, the Bank estimated that 21 percent of the population of the world's developing nations lived in extreme poverty, a total of 1.1 billion people, a reduction from 1.2 billion in 1990 and 1.5 billion in 1981.

Over the past three decades, regional trends in the international poverty rate (figure 6.1) indicate that the poverty rate has declined dramatically in most of Asia, has increased in Africa and in the countries of the former Soviet Union, and has held relatively constant throughout the Middle East and Latin America. The most dramatic reductions in poverty have been in India and China. In China alone, 400 million fewer people lived in poverty in 2001 than did so in 1980, with most of the decline occurring in the early 1980s. Although the poverty rate for sub-Saharan Africa has increased only marginally, the number of poor persons in that region nearly doubled, from 164 million to 316 million.[4]

Poverty is just one of several indicators reported in the World Bank's annual *World Development Report,* a widely respected source of statistical informa-

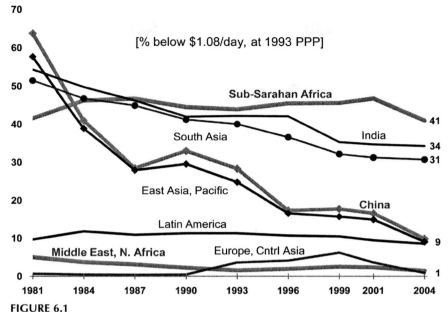

FIGURE 6.1
World Regional Trends in Extreme Poverty, 1981–2001
Source: World Bank, PovcalNet, http://iresearch.worldbank.org/PovcalNet/jsp/index.jsp.

tion on trends in poverty and related social conditions.[5] In the report, and on its website, the Bank presents detailed information on national accounts (e.g., GDP, national income, and trade data), business conditions, governmental policies, and developmental assistance. The United Nations provides similar data on its website and in a series of annual and regional *Human Development Reports*.[6] Although much of the data is the same, the tone of the two reports reflects the ideologies of the countries in control of the organizations. The World Bank tends to see poverty as something to be addressed by economic development; the United Nations stresses that alleviating poverty and inequality will have the side benefit of promoting economic development.

In 2000, the United Nations adopted the Millennium Declaration, setting eight broad development goals for developing nations relating to various aspects of poverty, education, gender inequality, health, and environment (table 6.1). Forty-eight development indicators, including the $1 a day poverty rate, are used to measure progress toward the goals. For poverty, the goal is to reduce the $1 poverty rate by half, from nearly 28 percent in 1990 to 14 percent in 2015. Although much of the developing world has made significant progress toward achieving these goals, in Africa conditions have stagnated or gotten worse on many indicators.

TABLE 6.1
Millennium Development Goals: Selected Indicators*

	1990	2001	2015 Goals
Developing Nations			
Poverty rate	27.9	21.3	14
Undernourishment rate	20.0	17.0	10
School enrollment	79.5	82.2	100
—girls	73.2	79.5	100
—boys	85.5	85.5	100
Literacy gender parity index	88	91	100
Child death rate	105	88	34
Sub-Saharan Africa			
Poverty rate	44.6	46.4	22
Undernourishment rate	36.0	33.0	18
School enrollment	53.9	62.2	100
—girls	49.8	58.5	100
—boys	58.0	65.8	100
Literacy gender parity index	80.0	88.0	100
Child death rate	185	179	61
HIV rates	2.7	7.3	(reverse the trend)

*Poverty: % of population below $1 a day level
Undernourishment: % of adults undernourished
School enollment: % of primary school aged children enrolled
Literacy gender parity index: ratio of women's to men's rates, age 15–24
Child death rate: under 5 deaths per 1,000 live births
HIV rate: % aged 15 to 49 with HIV
Source: United Nations Department of Economic and Social Affairs, "Progress towards the Millennium Development Goals, 1990-2005," 6/13/2005.

It is generally the position of the World Bank and the International Monetary Fund (IMF) that free market reforms and addressing political corruption will provide the solutions to poverty in the developing world. African countries generally rank among the world's poorest nations and their governments typically rank as the most corrupt, as measured by Transparency International's Corruption Perceptions Index.[7]

Poorer nations tend to be more corrupt than wealthy nations (figure 6.2), but whether political corruption is the cause or the effect of poverty is a matter of much dispute. Bob Geldof, activist and organizer of the Live Aid and Live 8 concerts, argues that "Africa is not mired in corruption, it is mired in poverty. Corruption is a by-product of poverty, just like dying of famine or Aids."[8] The free market policies advocated by the World Bank and the IMF are also subject of much controversy. Critics of the World Bank and the IMF argue that the organizations' advocacy of market reforms—such as privatization, reduced government subsidies, free trade and business deregulation—re-

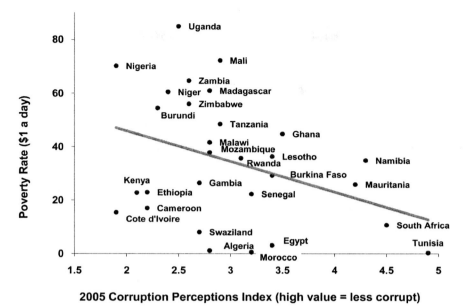

FIGURE 6.2
Corruption and Poverty in African Nations
Sources: World Bank, PovcalNet; Transparency International, http://www.transparency.org/.

sult in reductions in necessary social services and increased poverty and inequality.

The dramatic reductions in East and South Asian poverty (shown in figure 6.1) since the 1980s can be credited to free market reforms in China and India. On the other hand, the rising levels of extreme poverty in the former Soviet bloc (Eastern Europe and Central Asia) also followed the market reforms after the fall of communism.[9]

In Latin America, where poverty rates have remained steady for the past two decades, only two countries have managed to achieve substantial reductions in poverty: Chile and Guyana (figure 6.3). Both of these countries have pursued aggressive free market economic policies, in the case of Guyana under the impetus of IMF/World Bank structural adjustment policies.

Issues of Data Reliability

While both the United Nations and World Bank strive to provide accurate and reliable measures of poverty and other social and economic indicators, much

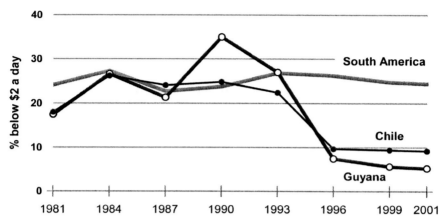

South America: Argentina, Bolivia, Brazil, Colombia,
Ecuador, Paraguay, Peru, Uruguay, Venezuela

FIGURE 6.3
Poverty Rates in Chile, Guyana, and South America
Sources: World Bank, PovcalNet.

of the data is of uncertain quality. Many of the poorest nations—such as Zimbabwe or the Democratic Republic of the Congo—lack the bureaucratic infrastructure to conduct accurate demographic counts and those poor nations with large government bureaucracies may produce data designed merely to make the bureaucracies look good.

Constructing the poverty measure involves two steps: determining the distribution of income (or consumption) across a country's households (i.e., how many households live at each income level), and defining what the $1 and $2 a day standard means in local currency. In the case of the World Bank's poverty measure, the base data are derived from national surveys of household consumer expenditure or income conducted at widely varying intervals in each country: approximately every six years in India, annually or biennially in China, rarely or never in many of the poorest nations. Typically, the household consumption survey asks a member of the household to report the household's food consumption and other purchases over the previous week or month. The data are then extrapolated into yearly figures. The base data provide estimates of the percentage of households living at each level of consumption or income and are used to estimate the poverty rate using national standards and to generate measures of economic growth and income distribution (such as the Gini coefficient or Lorenz curve).

Next, one has to determine what level of national consumer expenditure corresponds to the World Bank's $1 and $2 a day standards. Because a U.S.

dollar may not buy the same amount of consumer goods in each country, an estimate of the purchasing power parity of each country's national currency are used. The measurement requires additional household surveys to determine what commodities people in the country typically consume and retail business surveys to detail the price of those commodities. The consumer price surveys are similar to those used to estimate consumer inflation in the United States, but where the United States conducts the surveys every month and releases the results within a month, the World Bank' estimates take much longer. As of late 2007, the Bank has yet to finalize the PPP data from its most recent survey, conducted in 2005.

The methods of collecting, and the quality of consumption and price data, can vary wildly from country to country and cross-country and time-series comparisons of the data are often highly suspect. In many countries, the local population may be highly suspicious of governmental officials who come asking questions, while in others survey forms may be completed by enumerators who never leave their offices.

The estimates of world and regional poverty (shown in figure 6.1) are indirect measures based on the available country reports and other measures of economic growth. When household survey data are not available but general national income measures are, the Bank uses estimates based on the assumption that the income distribution is the same as in similar neighboring countries. To estimate the poverty rates for years when there were no household surveys, the Bank assumes all income levels have increased or decreased at the national growth rate.[10] Thus, the estimates report reductions in poverty whenever a country experiences national economic growth. This makes the data highly suspect for scholars who argue that globalization and international investment produce uneven economic growth.

Measuring Poverty in Wealthy Nations

When the World Bank estimates the total world population living below the $1 a day level, it makes the reasonable assumption that almost no one in the developed world would fall below the standard. In the United States, a family receiving food stamps would easily exceed the $2 a day consumption standard. Beginning in 1983, the Luxembourg Income Study (LIS) began compiling a collection of household income surveys conducted (usually) annually by many of the world's wealthiest countries. The LIS database now includes income surveys from twenty-nine countries. Under the direction of Timothy Smeeding and Lee Rainwater, the LIS center adjusts the national survey data to provide for consistent measures of income distribution and poverty across nations.

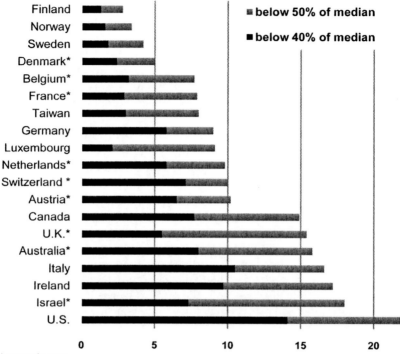

% of Children Living in Families with Incomes below
40% and 50% of Median Family Income

FIGURE 6.4
Child Poverty in Rich Nations, 2000
Source: Luxembourg Income Study, http://www.lisproject.org/keyfigures.htm.

Unlike the World Bank poverty measures, the poverty indicator most commonly reported by the LIS is a relative measure: the percentage of persons living
in families earning below 50 percent (or some other percentage) of the national
median family income, adjusted for family size (figure 6.4). Unlike the U.S. measure, the LIS measure is based on disposable income (income after taxes) and includes some "near-cash" income, such as (in the U.S. case) food stamps.

Smeeding and Rainwater have used these data in a series of reports and a
book addressing international differences in child poverty, calling attention to
the consistently highest rates of child poverty in the United States (figure 6.4).[11]

Note, however, that the high rate of child poverty is based on a relative
threshold measure of poverty and the United States has the highest median
family income of the nations shown. Nevertheless, high relative poverty in the

United States does point to a disturbing economic phenomenon, especially for a country that has always thought of itself as a middle-class society. Other analyses of the LIS data also consistently find that the United States has the highest levels of income inequality among wealthy Organisation for Economic Co-operation and Development (OECD) nations.[12]

Measuring Poverty in the United States

In 1963, Molly Orshansky, an economist at the Social Security Administration, undertook the task of determining just how many people in the United States were poor.[13] Although conservative and liberal scholars have debated the merits of the indicator ever since, the U.S. poverty rate statistic that she developed remains today as one of the most commonly used measures of the nation's economic health.

To measure the poverty rate, it was first necessary to determine the threshold for classifying families as poor. Orshansky began with studies of food budgets conducted by the Department of Agriculture in the mid-1950s. The U.S. Department of Agriculture (USDA) had developed an Economy Food Plan, a budget designed to meet the basic nutritional needs of families. In 1963, the Economy Food Plan cost a family of four (two adults and two children) an average of $1,033 per year. A separate 1955 study of family budgets had determined that American families (all families) spent an average of one-third of their budget on food. Multiplying the food budget by three, Orshansky set $3,100 as the poverty threshold for a family of four.

The threshold is adjusted for family size and for changes in the Consumer Price Index (note: not for changes in cost of the food budget). For 2006, the resulting poverty threshold for a family of four stood at $20,614. Persons living in four person families where the total family income was less than $20,614 were classified as poor and those with higher incomes are classified as not poor. In 2006, 37 million Americans were living in poor families, 12.6 percent of the total population (7.7 million families were poor, 9.9 percent of the families).

The U.S. poverty rate fell sharply in the 1960s, reaching its lowest point in 1973, and has fluctuated in a narrow range since then (figure 6.5). Poverty trends generally reflect changes in the economy: the declines in the 1990s reflect the economic prosperity of the Clinton administration years, and the increases before and after those years, the economic downturns of the two Bush administrations.

The Bureau of Labor Statistics and the Census Bureau derive income and poverty estimates from the annual March Current Population Survey (CPS),

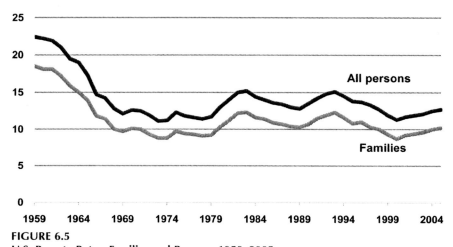

FIGURE 6.5
U.S. Poverty Rates: Families and Persons, 1959–2005
Source: U.S. Census Bureau, Poverty Historical Tables, http://www.census.gov/hhes/www/poverty/
   poverty.html.

based on a national sample of approximately 77,000 families. Although in comparison to many other surveys and polls, this is a very large sample size with a relatively high response rate, the sample size is often not large enough to provide reliable data for small demographic groups or regions. For the U.S. population as a whole, the sampling error (based on a 90 percent confidence interval) is approximately plus or minus .2 percent. Thus, if the reported poverty rate is 11.8 percent, we can be 90 percent sure that the true rate is between 11.6 and 12.0 percent. For subpopulations in the survey (e.g., children, or two-parent households) the sampling errors are greater, depending on the sample size. Since 2000, the Census Bureau has provided additional poverty estimates based on its continuous year-round American Community Survey. In 2006, this survey had a sample size of three million addresses, providing reliable poverty estimates for all states and areas with a population greater than 65,000.

Because the CPS survey includes many demographic questions about age, family structure and marital status, race, and ethnicity, the data allow for very detailed analysis of the demographics of poverty. In figure 6.6, for example, we see that much of the disparity in black and white family poverty (but not Hispanic and white) can be accounted for by the differences in family structure.

Senator Daniel Moynihan (D-NY) often called attention to the disparity in trends in poverty rates for children and the elderly.[14] In the 1960s, poverty

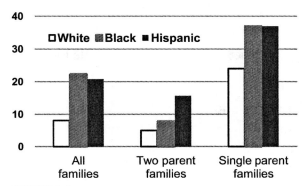

FIGURE 6.6
Family Poverty Rates by Race, Ethnicity, and Family
Structure, 2003
Source: U.S. Census Bureau, Poverty Historical Tables.

rates fell for both groups, but after the early 1970s, the child poverty rate began to increase while the elderly poverty rate continued to decline—to the point where the elderly are now less likely to be poor than the population as a whole (figure 6.7). These trends, Moynihan argued, were the result of the substantial increases in Social Security and Supplemental Security Income benefits for the elderly after 1970 and the steady decline in funding for Aid to Families with Dependent Children and other programs that targeted families with

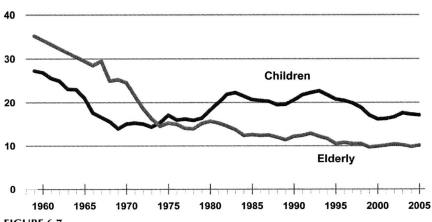

FIGURE 6.7
Poverty Rates for Children and Elderly, 1959–2005
Source: U.S. Census Bureau, Poverty Historical Tables.

children. By implication, the failure of Congress to enact a welfare reform plan Moynihan authored for the Nixon administration in 1969 was largely to blame.

Problems with the Poverty Statistics

There have been many complaints that the poverty statistics either overestimate or underestimate the true poverty rate. Liberals say that poverty is higher than the numbers indicate while conservatives insist that the numbers exaggerate the poverty rate—although these claims are made more or less strenuously, depending on which party is in power.

Liberals often complain that the poverty thresholds are too low. Although food was one-third of a family budget in the 1950s, it is one-seventh now. Considering this, they insist, would call for a higher threshold.[15] In addition, poverty thresholds are adjusted for price inflation, rather than income. Because incomes generally rise faster than prices, the poverty thresholds are much lower today compared to the average family income than they were in the 1960s. Poverty measures also do not fully capture what we mean by poverty. Families with incomes above the poverty line may nevertheless be deeply in debt, often because of large medical bills.

Conservatives argue that the thresholds are set too high in part because the Consumer Price Index used to adjust the poverty threshold has been shown to exaggerate the level of inflation as much as 1 percent per year. They also note that the definition of "money income" used in the measure does not include noncash income such as food stamp benefits, public housing, or Medicaid benefits. Because the income measure is based on pretax income, it does not take into account the Earned Income Tax Credit (EITC) benefits that many working families with children receive.

Although there is some basis for both claims, one has to understand that poverty is an inherently subjective concept to begin with: there is no such thing as a true poverty rate. Most of the complaints about the poverty rate statistic concern its validity (whether the statistic measures what it is supposed to measure), but questions about the statistic's reliability (the consistency of the measurement) are often more to the point.

Consider the conclusion that might be drawn from the trends in child and elderly poverty rates in figure 6.7. Because families with children are much more likely to receive EITC and food stamp benefits, which are not counted as income, than are the elderly, the disparity is not as great as the data indicate. Also, because the EITC benefits were first offered in the 1980s and substantially increased in the first year of the Clinton administration, real child poverty has declined at a faster rate than the data show. In addition, because many of the elderly poor have savings and assets that do not enter into the calculation of their family income, the poverty rate statistic may overestimate their level of poverty.

Measuring Income Inequality

The income data used to derive the poverty measurements can also be used to address many other issues related to income inequality. Thus, figure 6.8 shows trends in the share of aggregate family income for the richest 5 percent of households and the poorest 40 percent. Since 1980, the wealthy have seen their share of family income steadily increase.

Note, however, that conservatives sometimes object that the income distribution data reflect changes in household composition: the highest income groups tend to comprise larger households than the lower income groupings. The top household income quintile (containing the wealthiest 20 percent of the nation's households), for example, includes 24.6 percent of the population in 2005, the bottom quintile, only 14.3 percent.[16]

Other research on income and poverty relies on data obtained from the Panel Study of Income Dynamics conducted by the Institute for Social Research at the University of Michigan. Unlike most social indicator surveys, the panel study interviews the same families each year (or biennially), permitting analyses of the duration of poverty status and welfare participation. Using

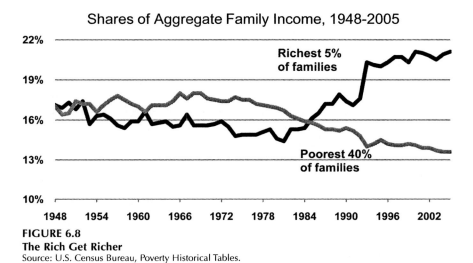

FIGURE 6.8
The Rich Get Richer
Source: U.S. Census Bureau, Poverty Historical Tables.

TABLE 6.2
Income Mobility in the 1970s and 1990s

Where Families Started, by Quintile	Where Families Ended up 10 Years Later, by Quintile				
	Poorest	Second	Third	Fourth	Richest
1969					
Poorest	**49.4**	24.5	13.8	9.1	3.3
Second	23.2	**27.8**	25.2	16.2	7.7
Third	10.2	23.4	**24.8**	23.0	18.7
Fourth	9.9	15.0	24.1	**27.4**	23.7
Richest	5.0	9.0	13.2	23.7	**49.1**
1988					
Poorest	**53.3**	23.6	12.4	6.4	4.3
Second	25.7	**36.3**	22.6	11	4.3
Third	10.9	20.7	**28.3**	27.5	12.6
Fourth	6.5	12.9	23.7	**31.1**	25.8
Richest	3.0	5.7	14.9	23.2	**53.2**

Source: Bradbury and Katz, "Are Lifetime Incomes Growing More Unequal?" 5.

these data, Katherine Bradbury and Jane Katz report evidence that income mobility declined in the United States in the 1990s: families were more likely to remain in the same "income quintile" than they were in the past (table 6.2).[17] The odds of the poor remaining poor and the rich remaining rich were higher in 1988 than in 1969.

Spinning the Income and Poverty Statistics

In addition to the poverty measures, the Current Population Survey provides several different indicators of income and earnings. The choice of indicators and the indicators' base (whether persons, families, or households) can lead to different conclusions, and comparisons of the different measures can lead to even more insightful conclusions, but readers should be aware that the choices provide many opportunities to cherry pick the data.[18] Next we will examine two arguments using the poverty and income data, one liberal and one conservative, to demonstrate how data selection can shape the authors' conclusions.

On the liberal side, we will consider just a piece of a larger argument made by *New York Times* columnist Paul Krugman in his 2007 book, *The Conscience of a Liberal*. Krugman's main argument is that conservative tax and social policies since the Reagan administration have produced a level of social and economic inequality in America little different from that of the pre-Depression-

TABLE 6.3
Measures of Income Change, 1973–2005*

	1973	2005	% Change
Per capita income	$12,204	$25,036	105
Mean household income	46,268	63,344	37
Median household income	40,008	46,326	16
Median earnings, men**	42,573	41,386	−3
Median personal income:			
men, ages 35–44**	45,785	40,964	−11
women ages, 35–44**	15,642	25,435	63

*In constant 2005 dollars.
**Full-time year-round workers.
Source: U.S. Census Bureau, *Historical Income Tables*, tables H10, P1, P8, P38.

era Gilded Age. Much of his argument is based on evidence, such as that presented in figure 6.8, of rising income inequality since the early 1980s.

A small part of Krugman's argument is a claim that the typical American family has made little if any economic progress over these years.[19] In presenting his evidence, Krugman employs several different income measures and takes great care to present his numerical evidence in terms general readers can understand. He begins by conceding that America is indeed a wealthier nation: "average income—the total income of the nation, divided by the number of people—has gone up substantially since 1973, the last year of the great boom."[20]

Krugman does not cite the actual data, but he is correct: since 1973, per capita income in constant dollars has increased 105 percent. Average, or mean, household income has not increased quite as fast, only 37 percent, because households have become smaller. (Table 6.3 contains the data, and more, that Krugman seems to be referring to.) Krugman attributes the increase to the growth in productivity spurred largely by the technological advances of the era. He notes, however, that the average income is not a valid measure of how well most people are doing. "If Bill Gates walks into a bar," he explains, "the average wealth of the bar's clientele soars, but the men already there when he walked in are no wealthier than before." The better indicator, he writes, would be the median income (half the incomes are above and half are below the median). When Gates walks into a bar, the median income hardly changes at all.[21]

Here, Krugman finds that "median household income adjusted for inflation, grew modestly from 1973 to 2005. . . . The total gain was about 16 percent." Krugman evaluates this evidence and concedes (commendably) that in some respects the 16 percent increase may understate the true increase in prosperity, as inflation adjustments may overstate the true inflation rate and do not capture the improvements in the quality of products that today's dollar can buy.

On the other hand, he notes that the household income growth has been achieved mostly by more Americans working and working longer hours. The increase in women entering the workforce has been a good thing, Krugman says, "but a gain in family income that occurs because a spouse goes to work is not the same thing as a wage increase." He points out that the earnings of men working year-round full-time have actually declined since 1973 (the 3 percent decline in table 6.3) and that when we compare men of the same age, the decline is even greater: "If we look at the earnings of men aged thirty-five to forty-four—men who would a generation ago often support stay-at-home wives—we find that the inflation-adjusted wages were 12 percent *higher* in 1973 than they are now."[22]

Krugman finally concludes that "the typical American family hasn't made clear progress in the last thirtysomething years."[23] Here, Krugman's conclusion rests on a careful but one-sided presentation of the evidence. It is true that the typical household has not made clear progress, but only if you mean the typical 1973 household. In 1973, there were three persons in the United States for every household. By 2005 that had declined to a little over two and one-half. The men and stay-at-home wives who supported a family in 1973 are supporting smaller families today, often with two incomes. Moreover, women's earnings have risen substantially over the same period, but Krugman does not mention that women aged thirty-five to forty-four have seen their inflation-adjusted income increase 63 percent.

Krugman precisely defines his indicators using the exact Census Bureau terminology, allowing this reader to verify the accuracy of the statistics (and, thus, to construct table 6.3). He makes critical distinctions in interpreting alternative measures of income and acknowledges the limitations of at least some of his data, but he leaves out some critical evidence that does not fit his conclusion.

As one-sided as Krugman's presentation of the evidence is, it is the very model of a fair and balanced presentation when considered alongside the following statistical argument from the other side of the political spectrum.

It took place in an exchange between talk show host Bill O'Reilly and "Larry," one of his radio show callers:

CALLER: Hi, Bill.

O'REILLY: Larry.

CALLER: Let's see, poverty is up since Bush took office.

O'REILLY: That's not true.

CALLER: It is true.

O'REILLY: I have the stats right here, Larry.

CALLER: I just looked at the figures. Gun crime is up since George Bush took office.

O'REILLY: All right, Larry, hold it, hold it, hold it. Let's deal with one at a time. The only fair comparison is halfway through Clinton's term, halfway through Bush's term, Okay? That's the only fair comparison. You gotta go real time.

CALLER: Bill, I —

O'REILLY: Poverty is down, Larry, one full percent in real time from 1996, halfway through Clinton 2004, halfway through Bush. That is the truth, Larry, and if you're not willing to acknowledge that's the truth, this conversation is over.[24]

O'Reilly's claim, that I heard repeated on two "no-spin zone" Fox News cable TV broadcasts, is based on two entirely accurate statistics combined with a lot of very faulty reasoning. O'Reilly's statistics are accurate: Bush's fourth year poverty rate was a full percent lower than Clinton's fourth year poverty rate (figure 6.9). And O'Reilly's interpretation of the two numbers involves what seems like a reasonable premise: it would be unfair to compare what President Bush has achieved in four years with what President Clinton achieved over eight years. Nevertheless, O'Reilly is unwilling to acknowledge that Larry is also telling the truth and providing a better interpretation of the data. Where O'Reilly goes wrong is in using the rate at the end of the first term rather than the change in the rate over the presidents' four years in office: the poverty rate went down 1.2 percentage points in Clinton's first term and up 1.4 percentage points in Bush's first term. And it fell another 2.4 points in Clinton's second term. Viewed another way, O'Reilly gives Bush credit for all of the decline in the poverty rate since the midpoint of Clinton's term in

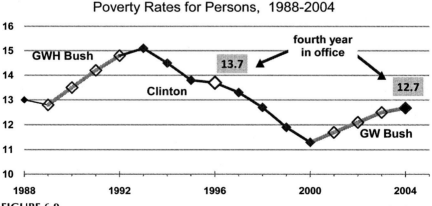

FIGURE 6.9
How President Bush Lowered the Poverty Rate
Source: U.S. Census Bureau, Poverty Historical Tables.

office, but all of that decline, and more, took place while Clinton was in office. As Senator Moynihan might have said, you're entitled to your own opinion, Mr. O'Reilly, but not to your own facts.

It is not true what they say: "You can prove anything you want with statistics." It is true that you can find and/or present statistics in support of just about any claim, but it takes more than just the statistics to reach any conclusion. To "prove" something with statistics usually takes at least two things: the statistics and some thinking. When people make bogus claims about numbers, it is usually the thinking, not the statistics, that is at fault.

Notes

1. Michel Chossudovsky, "Global Falsehoods: How the World Bank and the UNDP Distort the Figures on Global Poverty," The Transnational Foundation for Peace and Future Research, 1999, at http://www.transnational.org/SAJT/features/chossu_worldbank.html; Garth L. Mangum, Stephen L. Mangum, and Andrew M. Summ, *The Persistence of Poverty in the United States* (Baltimore, Md.: Johns Hopkins University Press, 2003).

2. Robert Rector and Rea Hederman, Jr. "Two Americas: One Rich, One Poor? Understanding Income Inequality in the United States," The Heritage Foundation backgrounder #1791, August 24, 2004, at www.heritage.org/Research/Taxes/bg1791.cfm.

3. In order to make the standards close to the national poverty standards of a set of nations, the actual standards are $1.08 and $2.15 a day.

4. Shaohua Chen and Martin Ravallion, "How Have the World's Poorest Fared since the Early 1980s?" Policy Research Working Paper 3341 (Washington, D.C.: World Bank, 2000) at ideas.repec.org/p/wbk/wbrwps/3341.html.

5. World Bank, *World Development Report 2007: Development and the Next Generation* (Washington, D.C.: World Bank, 2006).

6. United Nations Development Programme, *Human Development Report 2006: Beyond Scarcity: Power, Poverty and the Global Water Crisis* (New York: UNDP, 2006) at hdr.undp.org/hdr2006.

7. Transparency International, *Global Corruption Report 2007* (Cambridge: Cambridge University Press, 2007).

8. BBC News, "G8 Leaders 'Real Stars of Show,'" July 2, 2005, at news.bbc.co.uk/2/hi/uk_news/4643451.stm.

9. Jeffrey Sachs, *The End of Poverty: Economic Possibilities for Our Time* (New York: Penguin Press, 2005).

10. Sanjay G. Reddy and Thomas W. Pogge, "How Not to Count the Poor" Version 6.2, 2005, at www.columbia.edu/~sr793/count.pdf.

11. Lee Rainwater and Timothy M. Smeeding, *Poor Kids in a Rich Country: America's Children in Comparative Perspective* (New York: Russell Sage Foundation, 2003).

12. Timothy M. Smeeding, "Public Policy, Economic Inequality, and Poverty: The United States in Comparative Perspective," *Social Science Quarterly* 86, no. s1 (2005): 955–83.

13. Gordon M. Fisher. "The Development of the Orshansky Poverty Thresholds and Their Subsequent History as the Official U.S. Poverty Measure," U.S. Census Bureau—Poverty Measurement Working Papers, 1997, at www.census.gov/hhes/poverty/povmeas/papers/orshansky.html.

14. Daniel Patrick Moynihan, *Family and Nation* (New York: Harcourt Brace Janovich, 1987).

15. Garth L. Mangum, Stephen L. Mangum, and Andrew M. Sum, *The Persistence of Poverty in the United States* (Baltimore, Md.: Johns Hopkins University Press, 2003), 81. The argument does not take into account that the threshold has been adjusted upward for inflation in all consumer goods, not just for increases in food prices.

16. Rector and Hederman, "Two Americas: One Rich, One Poor?"

17. Katharine Bradbury and Jane Katz, "Are Lifetime Incomes Growing More Unequal?" *Regional Review*, Quarter 4 (2002): 3–5 at www.bos.frb.org/economic/nerr/rr2002/q4/issues.pdf.

18. A household consists a person or group sharing the same housing unit. A family, or more precisely a family household, consists of two or more related persons in the same housing unit.

19. Paul Krugman, *The Conscience of a Liberal* (New York: W. W. Norton, 2007), 124–28.

20. Krugman, *The Conscience of a Liberal*, 125.

21. Krugman, *The Conscience of a Liberal*, 125.

22. Note that Krugman says 1973 wages were 12 percent higher than 2005 wages, but table 6.3 shows an 11 percent decline in income from 1973 to 2005. Both numbers are correct: Krugman is using the 2005 data as his divisor. I am assuming "wages" refers to the median income measure, as this is most consistent with the numbers he reports. Krugman, *The Conscience of a Liberal*, 127.

23. Krugman, *The Conscience of a Liberal*, 128.

24. Media Matters for America, "O'Reilly Defended False Clinton–Bush Poverty Comparison as 'the Only Accurate Measuring Stick,'" September 16, 2005, at media-matters.org/items/200509160002.

7

Finding the Data

THIS CONCLUDING CHAPTER WILL ADDRESS what is logically the first stage of any data-based research project: before you present and interpret your data, you have to find them. The chapter comes at the end because a productive data search best begins with a clear understanding of what kind of data are likely to be available and how other investigators have used the available data to define and address the critical questions one might wish to study. A subtext of what precedes this chapter has been to share with the reader an understanding of the variety and wealth of social indicator data that are available from governmental and nongovernmental sources for those who would use numerical evidence to address questions of public policy and political affairs. This chapter will take that a step further, offering a more detailed description of the data sources used for this book and the other data that are available from these and related sources.

Almost all social indicators in this book—with the exception of data derived from agency records such as the FBI Uniform Crime Report and the U.S. Federal Budget—were originally derived from surveys, usually regular periodic surveys, conducted by either a governmental agency or a survey organization. Each indicator was first constructed from "raw" data files containing each individual response to the questions in the surveys. Thus, the Census Bureau calculates monthly employment indicators, annual poverty and income estimates, and biennial voter turnout measures from the raw responses to its monthly Current Population Survey.

Much of the data used in the charts and tables in this book was obtained from the primary sources, often from the Census Bureau or statistical agency websites. In some cases secondary sources were used either to demonstrate how particular researchers used the data, because some secondary sources have improved on the raw data, or because the data were more conveniently formatted by the secondary source. Many publications and websites repackage primary source data, combining data from different sources on related topics in ways that provide added value for researchers. On education, for example, the journal *Education Week* produces an annual publication and database, *Quality Counts,* that reports a series of indicators on state educational achievement, school climate, state policies, and fiscal resources. The journal also scores states on several indexes related to school finance and student achievement.[1] Similarly, the annual *Kids Count Data Book* provides a similar compilation of data on the status of American children.[2]

Some data were not available on any statistical website but were obtained from published research articles and, in one case, by requesting that the author of a published study forward a copy of the data. Finding data on the timing of state and national laws is a particularly challenging task. For the analysis of Election Day registration in chapter 4, the information was provided through a published study and an Internet search that revealed the timing of Oregon's law. To fill in missing data on the civil registries in Greece and Luxembourg, I phoned the Luxembourg embassy in Washington, D.C. and e-mailed a graduate school friend working with a Greek political campaign organization.

For most research endeavors, a good literature review is not only essential to defining the critical issues but also reveals crucial information on the kinds of data and the primary data sources that have been used to address the issue in the past. Using both library and Internet search engines, I have often found it useful to include the words "table" or "figure" with the search terms to find data-based research studies.

General Data Sources

The *U.S. Statistical Abstract*

The *U.S. Statistical Abstract,* published annually by the Census Bureau since 1878, serves as a comprehensive source for American social indicator data and as a reference guide to a wide variety of U.S. governmental, international, and a few private data sources.[3] The 2007 edition of the *Abstract* contains 1,376 data tables organized by thirty topical chapters (such as Population, Vital Statistics, Elections, Education, Agriculture, and Foreign Commerce). Each chapter begins with a general discussion of the data, how the data were collected, and the reliability and validity of the primary data sources.

The *Statistical Abstract* website (www.census.gov/compendia/statab) contains every edition of the *Abstract*, downloadable in Adobe .pdf format. The website for the 2007 edition contains each chapter of the printed edition downloadable in .pdf format and links to spreadsheet files for each of the *Abstract*'s tables. The spreadsheet files often contain more data than is shown in the printed edition (for previous editions, these spreadsheet files were available on a CD-Rom). This is especially true of tables containing time series data. The historical poverty and income data in the printed *Abstract* tables, for example, covers the years from 1980 to 2005, while the spreadsheet files contain annual data back to the beginning of the income series in 1959. Note, however, that the *Abstract*'s data can be as much as a year old and the primary agency website will contain both the most recently released data and more detailed tabulations. Most of the printed *Abstract* tables indicate the original agency providing the data and the files contain direct links to the agency websites.

Federal Statistical Agencies

Almost every federal department, and many federal agencies, have a statistical bureau or agency website providing program operations data (such as characteristics of the targeted population of the agency's programs), performance indicators (educational achievement data, highway fatality data), data collected from ongoing agency surveys, and data published in special studies and reports (see table 7.1). Many of the statistical agency websites also provide related international data and contain studies and reports addressing the reliability and validity of the data the department collects. The Fedstats.gov website (www.fedstats.gov) provides a comprehensive set of links to federal agency statistics, organized alphabetically by topic.

The Organisation for Economic Co-operation and Development (OECD)

The OECD is an international organization of thirty nations and is the best source of comparable international social indicator data for the world's developed democracies. The data include a broad range of economic indicators, government finance and program statistics, and education and health care data. Most convenient are the data provided through the SourceOECD website (www.sourceoecd.org), a subscription service available through many colleges and universities, in predefined spreadsheet tables or in tables created through an interactive database query. The OECD provides free access to "frequently requested data" and the data contained in its main statistical reports (*The OECD in Figures, The OECD Factbook, Society at a Glance,* and *Education*

TABLE 7.1
Key Federal Statistical Agencies

Department/Agency	Statistical Agency website	Data Provided
Agriculture	National Agricultural Statistics Service www.nass.usda.gov	Agricultural commodities production and prices; 5-year Census of Agriculture.
Commerce	Bureau of Economic Analysis www.bea.gov	International trade and investment, GDP, national income and product accounts, personal income, corporate profits.
	Economics and Statistics Administration www.esa.doc.gov	GDP and national accounts data, economic sector production and sales.
	Census Bureau www.census.gov	Decennial population census, annual *Current Population Survey*, income and economic statistics, international trade.
Defense	Statistical Information Analysis Division siadapp.dmdc.osd.mil	Armed Forces personnel, casualties, procurement.
Education	National Center for Education Statistics nces.ed.gov	Comprehensive source for almost all education data.
Energy	Energy Information Administration eia.doe.gov	Nuclear, electricity, coal, natural gas, and petroleum production.
Environmental Protection Agency	Environmental Protection Agency epa.gov	Environmental toxins, chemical releases, greenhouse gas emissions.
Federal Election Commission	Federal Election Commission fec.gov	Campaign finance.
Health and Human Services	National Center for Health Statistics cdc.gov/nchs	Vital Statistics (births, deaths, marriage and divorce), disease and health measures, health care system and health insurance.
Homeland Security	Office of Immigration Statistics dhs.gov/ximgtn/statistics	Legal immigration and naturalization.
Housing and Urban Development	Office of Policy Development & Research huduser.org	*American Housing Survey*, public housing, housing affordability.

Department/Agency	Statistical Agency website	Data Provided
Interagency	Interagency Forum on Child & Family Statistics childstats.gov	Census Bureau and other agency data dealing with children and families.
	Federal Interagency Forum on Aging-Related Statistics AgingStats.Gov	Federal aging statistical sources, annual *Older American Update*.
Interior	Bureau of Indian Affairs www.doi.gov/bureau-indian-affairs.html	The BIA website is currently unavailable due to a lawsuit concerning the agency's mismanagement of Indian trust assets.
Internal Revenue Service	Statistics of Income Division www.irs.gov/taxstats/	Federal personal and corporate income tax data.
Justice	Bureau of Justice Statistics ojp.usdoj.gov/bjs/	Crime, criminal victims, and judicial system operations; death penalty and incarceration data.
	Federal Bureau of Investigation fbi.gov	Uniform Crime Reports, Hate Crime Statistics.
Labor	Bureau of Labor Statistics bls.gov	Employment, unemployment, consumer and producer prices.
President, office of	Office of Management & Budget whitehouse.gov/omb	The Federal Budget, see also: gpoaccess.gov/usbudget
Social Security Administration	Office of Policy ssa.gov/policy	Social Security and Medicare program data.
Transportation	National Center for Statistics and Analysis (NCSA) www.nhtsa.gov	Highway safety statistics.

at a Glance) through OECD.Stat, the OECD's central data warehouse at stats .oecd.org/wbos.

World Bank, International Monetary Fund, and United Nations

The World Bank, the International Monetary Fund (IMF) and the United Nations are primary sources of international financial, trade, social, and economic development indicators. Each provides some data concerning its own programs, such as IMF lending and financial data, and the organizations share much of the economic data. Although the United Nations data are freely accessible, the World Bank and IMF charge fees for access to some of their databases.

For data on developing countries, the World Bank provides for online queries of an archive of Millennium Development Goal indicators, international poverty estimates, and its *World Development Indicator* database (www.worldbank.org/data). The IMF provides access to the same data and data on international trade and commodity prices at www.imf.org/external/data.htm. The United Nations Statistics Division (unstats.un.org) provides access to data from three of its annual publications: *Demographic Yearbook, Population and Vital Statistics Report,* and *Human Development Report.* The *Human Development Report* database contains the most comprehensive set of indicators at hdr.undp.org/hdr2006/statistics.

Be warned that for many indicators on developing nations, particularly African nations, many of the social indicator data series have a great deal of missing data.

Public Opinion Polling Data

The Survey Documentation and Analysis center at the University of California, Berkeley, provides online database queries from two time series surveys: the American National Election Studies (ANES) survey, and the National Opinion Research Center's General Social Survey. The ANES survey, conducted every two years since 1948, contains a broad set of public opinion and political behavior questions asked in the biennial pre- and postelection surveys. The General Social Survey, conducted annually from 1972 to 1994 and biennially from 1994 to 2004, contains a wide range of social, political, behavioral, and demographic questions. To construct time series indicators from these datasets using the center's interface (sda.berkeley.edu), create a table by selecting "year" as the row variable and the relevant survey question as the column variable, specifying row percentages. The online query system also allows users to recode variables and to create demographic and other breakdowns of the questions.

Major polling organizations usually maintain online archives of at least the aggregate response tallies to questions asked in most of their regularly administered polls. For the most part, however, the organizations provide only limited public access to their data and require paid subscriptions to access the full archive. Of these, the Gallup organization's archive (www.galluppoll.com) provides access to the longest running and most comprehensive set of polls, often in a convenient time series format. Over one hundred American universities and colleges provide their students free access to the Roper Center for Public Opinion Research archives (www.ropercenter.uconn.edu) containing polling data from twenty-seven polling organizations in the form of question-level responses, some time series or "trended" survey response data, and raw datasets. More universities subscribe to the LexisNexis® Academic Universe, which provides single-question response data from a similar polling archive.

For online access to international surveys, see Political Participation in the following section on international data sources.

Notes on Data Sources Used in this Book

International Data

Corruption (figure 6.2)

Transparency International's *Corruption Perceptions Index* is compiled from surveys, conducted by other organizations, of international businesspeople and regional and country experts. Transparency International (www.transparency.org) also sponsors its own public survey on corruption in sixty-nine countries to calculate the *Global Corruption Barometer*, and surveys businesses in exporting countries to construct the *Bribes-Payer Index.*

Related cross-national indicators, employing a similar methodology, are Freedom House's (www.freedomhouse.org) annual index (since 1973) of political rights and civil liberties and the Heritage Foundation's (www.heritage.org) *Index of Economic Freedom,* an annual index (since 1995) based on measures of ten "economic freedoms" related to taxation, protection of private property, and economic regulation. Transparency International's *Corruption Perceptions Index* is one of the ten measures.

Education (figures 5.1–5.3 and tables 5.1–5.3)

The United States participates in several international educational achievement studies: the *Trends in International Mathematics and Science Study,* the *Progress in International Reading Literacy Study,* the OECD's *Program for International Student Assessment,* and the OECD's *Adult Literacy and Lifeskills Survey.* Each of these studies has its own website, but the U.S. National Center for Educational Statistics (nces.ed.gov) provides a single site containing the cross-national data for each of the surveys and evaluations of the survey methodology and data reliability. Generally, the data consist of both the national scores on the assessment tests and data on family background, student behavior, and school characteristics.

The OECD's annual publication *Education at a Glance* summarizes the results of the international tests and provides data on a variety of indicators related to school conditions, staffing, and finance. It is available through OECD's central data warehouse at stats.oecd.org/wbos/.

Global Warming (figure 1.2)

The Goddard Institute for Space Studies data (data.giss.nasa.gov) on global temperature anomalies is the most commonly cited evidence in the debates over global warming. The data are derived from worldwide meteorological station temperature records since the 1880s. The data measure departures from the normal monthly temperature at each station and are adjusted to account for localized urban warming, date, and time of day. The National Climatic Data Center at www.ncdc.noaa.gov provides the most extensive collection of global and regional weather data, including long-term reconstructions of historical temperature data, based on tree-ring analysis, and other methods.

Health Expenditures (figure 1.4 and table 1.1)

These data were obtained from the OECD's central data warehouse at stats.oecd.org/wbos.

Millennium Development Goals (table 6.1)

The World Bank's Global Data Monitoring Information System provides for online queries of its *Millennium Development Goals* (MDG) database (developmentgoals.org) and the United Nations provides for a similar data query of the forty-eight MDG indicators (mdgs.un.org).

Political Participation (figures 4.1, 4.2)

Since 1986, the International Social Survey Programme (ISSP) at www.issp .org has conducted annual cross-national surveys (for as many as thirty-nine nations) on topical issues including citizen participation, the environment, religion, social inequality, gender roles, and the role of government. The data in figure 4.2 were obtained using the site's online cross-tabular analysis of the survey data. To calculate country-level measures, cross-tabulate the country code id against a substantive variable.

The Comparative Study of Electoral Systems (CSES) website (www.cses .org) provides for similar online queries of cross-national national election surveys (including ANES 2004 data for the United States) for most of the OECD members, and a few other nations. At this writing, the site provides online tabulation only for election surveys conducted from 1996 to 2001. For similar general cross-national survey data, see the World Values Survey website at www.worldvaluessurvey.org.

Poverty—Developing Nations (figures 6.1–6.3)

The $1 and $2 a day poverty indicators are contained in the MDG databases, but the World Bank also provides somewhat more flexible database query access to regional and national poverty measures through its PovcalNet website at iresearch.worldbank.org/PovcalNet.

Poverty—Wealthy Nations (figures 3.10, 6.4)

The Luxembourg Income Survey compiles a variety of cross-national indicators related to income inequality and poverty using an archive of national income surveys obtained from thirty nations. It also provides cross-national data on wealth and characteristics of national social welfare programs (www.lisproject.org).

Voter Turnout and Election Systems (table 4.1)

The International Institute for Democracy and Electoral Assistance (IDEA) website (idea.int) is a good source of cross-national turnout data and information about national election systems, but the data have not yet been updated for elections after 2001. The IDEA also provides data on women's electoral participation and representation in national legislatures. The Administration and Cost of Elections Project provides a very comprehensive global survey of national election systems, including procedures for redistricting, voter registration, and vote counting (aceproject.org).

U.S. Data

Crime Rates (figures 1.5, 1.10–12 and table 1.5)

In addition to the National Crime Victimization Survey data used in several of the figures in chapter 1, the Bureau of Justice Statistics (BJS) provides a series of reports and data compilations on sentencing and imprisonment, capital punishment, drugs, and firearms. The BJS website seems to provide most of the FBI Uniform Crime Report data, although the FBI provides its data in a variety of formats. The FBI also collects hate crime statistics, but inconsistent local reporting of these crimes results in serious reliability problems.

Dow Jones Industrial Average (DJIA) (figure 3.29)

While the DJIA is the oldest and most recognized measure of stock market performance, it indexes the stock prices of only thirty companies. The Dow Jones Wilshire 5000 Composite Index is a much broader measure of stock market performance. The Yahoo! Finance website (finance.yahoo.com) is a convenient source of these and other stock market related data.

Educational Achievement—National Data (figures 5.5–5.9)

The National Center for Education Statistics (NCES) website provides several means of accessing National Assessment of Educational Progress (NAEP) data. Many NAEP tables are published in the annual *Condition of Education* and the NCES website provides access to all (over 400) tables in spreadsheet format. In addition, the NAEP Data Explorer, an online data-query tool, permits users to create their own tabulations from the NAEP database. The NCES's annual *Digest of Education Statistics* provides enrollment, staffing, finance, educational attainment, higher education, and international data.

Educational Achievement—State NCLB Data (figures 5.9–5.11 and table 5.3)

Except in the case of special reports (for example, figure 5.9), the NCES website does not provide access to the data derived from statewide No Child Left Behind (NCLB) testing. Generally, state NCLB data are made available on each state's department (or board) of education website. Commonly, the state websites provide easy access to individual school report cards containing school, school district, and state test scores, in addition to demographic and expenditure data. Using the larger files containing data for all the schools and school districts can be more cumbersome: just the codebook listing all the data items for the Illinois Report Card data file was several hundred pages long and the 2007 version of Excel (but not the 2003 version) had difficulty processing the large data file.

Education—Higher Education (figures 3.15–3.17)

The higher education data in chapter 3 were compiled by the Illinois Board of Higher Education and are readily available on the Board's website. Most states have similar governing boards for higher education, but the governance structure varies from state to state. Most multi-institution governing boards and most colleges and universities have an institutional research department responsible for compiling data and preparing reports on enrollments, tuition and fees, staffing, expenditures, and student academic performance. Often the data are presented in an annual data profile. The NCES provides some higher education data, mostly data concerning enrollments, tuition, and programs. Although American universities are currently going through an "assessment" fad, there are no reliable measures of educational achievement for higher education in the United States.

Federal Budgets (figures 1.8, 1.9 and 3.6, 3.8, 3.11, 3.14, 3.22, 3.23)

The president's Office of Management and Budget submits the proposed federal budget for each fiscal year (beginning October 1) to Congress in February of each year. The last section of the budget, the Historical Tables, contains an extensive set of time series tables, following the same table numbering and format in each year's volume. When using the federal budget data, be aware of the distinction between spending by function and by agency. Not all education spending, for example, is in the Department of Education's budget, some defense spending is in the Department of Energy budget, and the Department of Agriculture budget includes the food stamp program. Usually, the budget data defined by functional categories (function and subfunction) are more meaningful. The actual budget documents and spreadsheet files are available on the White House, the Office of Management and Budget, and the Government Printing Office websites.

Gas Prices (figure 3.29)

The Department of Energy's Energy Information Administration provides weekly gas price data and data related to all aspects of energy production and consumption. The agency's website also provides data on renewable energy sources and worldwide and international greenhouse gases and emissions.

Homeownership (figures 1.6, 1.7)

The Census Bureau conducts a decennial Census of Housing and also includes a series of questions on housing conditions and homeownership in its quarterly Current Population/Housing Vacancy Survey. The Census Bureau provides more convenient access to these data than does the Department of Housing and Urban Development.

Income (figure 6.8 and table 6.3)

Using a single set of responses to the March Current Population Survey, the Census Bureau calculates a large number of income-related economic indicators (and poverty data). Annual mean and median income (the broader measure), earnings, and wages-and-salary data are reported for households, families, full-time year-round workers, and all persons. The time series data are reported in current and constant (inflation adjusted) dollars.

Inflation (figures 1.2, 3.29)

The Bureau of Labor Statistics is the primary source for consumer and producer price indexes. The consumer price index measures price changes in a market basket of goods and services that consumers typically purchase and is often used to adjust monetary time series data to constant dollars. The Bureau also provides several related inflation indexes and measures for specific sectors of the economy, such as energy and retail food. Note that the inflation rate is a complex statistic and the indicator may underestimate or overestimate the true inflation rate in several different ways.[4] To adjust aggregate government expenditures for inflation, the Gross Domestic Product Deflator is the better measure. It is most conveniently found in the U.S. Budget Historical Tables, table 1.10.

The Misery Index (figure 1.1)

The Misery Index data used in figure 1.1 was obtained from a secondary website at miseryindex.us. The Bureau of Labor Statistics is the primary source of data for both unemployment and inflation.

National Debt (figure 1.9)

See the previous section on Federal Budgets.

Presidential Elections (figure 3.28)

The United States may be one of the few democracies where no single national governmental agency maintains official elections records, although the Federal Election Commission does maintain a database on campaign finance reports for federal elections and the Clerk of the House of Representatives does publish the vote counts (in a somewhat clumsy format) for each federal election since 1920. For the most part, official election records are maintained by each state's Secretary of State office. Congressional Quarterly, Inc., a privately owned publishing company, collects almost all of the data related to the votes-cast turnout measures and results of gubernatorial and federal elections, published in its biennial, *America Votes*.[5] The elections outcome data reported in the *U.S. Statistical Abstract* are mostly obtained from Congressional Quarterly, but the *Abstract* is the more accessible source of the data.

The Interuniversity Consortium for Political and Social Research's *United States Historical Election Returns* series contains congressional, presidential, and gubernatorial election return data at the state and county level for elections from 1788 through 1990. Many universities and colleges are members of the ICPSR, which provides an extensive library of raw data from surveys and research studies (www.icpsr.umich.edu).

Political Corruption (figures 3.25, 3.26)

Political corruption is generally not included among the crimes reported on the Bureau of Justice Statistics website. To obtain the state data on prosecution rates of public officials, I e-mailed one of the authors of the study cited, Kenneth Meier, and he graciously sent them to me. He developed the measure based on data obtained from an annual (since 1978) report submitted to the Congress by the Department of Justice Public Integrity Section, which details convictions for political corruption for each U.S. Attorney's office.[6] Of course, there is a fundamental validity question involved in using the "number of officials caught" as a measure of political corruption.

Poverty (figures 6.5–6.7, 6.9)

In addition to the annual March Current Population Survey (CPS) that has been used to measure income and poverty since 1959, income and poverty estimates are also derived from the decennial census and, since 1998, from the Census Bureau's monthly American Community Survey (ACS). The ACS is a much larger survey, sampling three million households each year, versus less than 100,000 for the CPS. Because the three surveys are conducted at different times of the year and use slightly different definitions of the target populations and adjustments for inflation, they produce slightly different estimates. ACS income estimates tend to be about 4 percent higher than those derived from the decennial census. The ACS also includes questions about housing, immigration, citizenship, and employment and will eventually replace the decennial census long-form questionnaire that has been administered to one out of six households.

Presidential Approval (figure 3.24)

The standard presidential approval ratings are based on one of two questions. Since 1937 the Gallup Poll has asked, "Do you approve or disapprove of the job [president's name] has done as president?" The alternative question, first used by the Harris Poll, asks, "How would you rate [president's name] performance on the job: excellent, good, fair or poor?" The many other polling firms now use one or the other, or a slight variation, on these questions. The Gallup Poll website has the most complete historical data on presidential approval and would be the best source for comparing several administrations' approval data, but access to their data requires a subscription fee. The most complete collection of presidential approval data for each administration, but not including Zogby data shown in figure 3.24, are available (for nonsubscribers) from the Roper Center website at www.ropercenter .uconn.edu. The Professor PollKatz Poll of Polls website (www.pollkatz .homestead.com/) contains time series charts (but not the actual data) on presidential approval surveys conducted by fifteen polling organizations. The Pollingreport.com website is also an excellent source for political polling data on upcoming state and national election races.

Unemployment (figures 1.1, 1.11 and 3.24, 3.29)

The Bureau of Labor Statistics provides a comprehensive set of monthly employment and unemployment statistics that are easily downloaded from their website. Note that the unemployment rate is a complex statistic with many issues involving the counts both of the workers and members of the labor force. The Bureau's publication "How the Government Measures Unemployment" provides an excellent summary of how the indicator is constructed.[7]

Social Capital Index (figures 3.25, 4.7)

The data for Robert Putnam's Social Capital Index are available online through the Interuniversity Consortium for Political and Social Research (ICPSR) at www.icpsr.umich.edu.

Voter Turnout—Voting Age Population Measures (figures 4.3–4.5)

The Census Bureau's postelection Current Population Survey data provide reported voter turnout data at the state level and for several demographic categories such as education, age, race, ethnicity, and gender. The data can be obtained from the Bureau's Voting and Registration website (census.gov/

population/www/socdemo/voting.html). The votes-cast measure are reported in the Statistical Abstract and obtained from the United States Elections Project website (elections.gmu.edu). In recent years, the Census Bureau has begun reporting turnout rates based on estimates of the voting age citizen population.

Voter Turnout—Voting Eligible Population Measures (figures 4.6, 4.7 and tables 4.2, 4.3)

Michael McDonald maintains the United States Elections Project website that provides detailed state-level data used in calculating the voter eligible turnout measures.

War Casualties (table 2.11)

The Iraq Casualties website (icasualties.org) provides accessible data on the Iraq War casualities and includes fatality data for the other coalition partners. It also includes, and documents, some casualty data based on news sources that the Defense Department has not yet confirmed. For official U.S. armed forces casualties, the Defense Department's Statistical Information Analysis Division (SIAD) Military Casualty Information website provides a considerable amount of data on U.S. war casualities going back to the Revolutionary War. For recent wars, the casualties are categorized by race, ethnicity, gender, service, home state, and circumstances.

Notes on Data Formats

The data from the statistical websites come in a variety of formats, even at a single agency website, and some agencies and websites make their social indicator data more accessible than others do. Ideally, the agency will provide the data in spreadsheet or a spreadsheet-compatible format (such as .csv), but data are also made available in web page (html) tables and in .pdf format. Data stored in a web page table easily transfers to a spreadsheet, by either cutting-and-pasting or by opening the URL address from the spreadsheet program. Some data are only available in Adobe .pdf files, particularly data contained in agency reports and research studies. The newest versions of the Adobe document viewer have some special features for copying tables and columns of data that work well with some tables but not others. Sometimes, all the columns from a .pdf data table (or data in plain text format on a web page) will "paste" into a single spreadsheet column. Depending on the table format, the "text to columns" function can often sort these data out.

Notes

1. "Quality Counts at 10: A Decade of Standards-Based Reform," *Education Week,* 25, no. 17 (January 5, 2006).

2. Annie E. Casey Foundation, *2007 Kids Count Data Book* (Baltimore, Md.: Annie E. Casey Foundation, 2007) at www.kidscount.org/sld/databook.jsp.

3. U.S. Census Bureau, *Statistical Abstract of the United States: 2007,* 126th ed., 2006, at www.census.gov/statab/www/.

4. Bureau of Labor Statistics, "Measurement Issues in the Consumer Price Index," June 1997, at www.bls.gov/cpi/cpigm697.htm.

5. Richard M. Scammon, Alice V. McGillivray, and Rhodes Cook, *America Votes 26: Election Returns by State, 2003–2004* (Washington, D.C.: Congressional Quarterly, 2005).

6. Public Integrity Section, Criminal Division, United States Department of Justice, "Report to Congress on the Activities and Operations of the Public Integrity Section for 2005," at www.usdoj.gov/criminal/pin/.

7. Bureau of Labor Statistics, "How the Government Measures Unemployment," July 2001, at www.bls.gov/cps/cps_htgm.htm.

Index

About the Author

Gary Klass is associate professor in the Department of Politics and Government at Illinois State University, where he teaches courses in quantitative research methods, public policy and race and ethnicity. He received his PhD in political science department from Binghamton University. He is past president of the of the American Political Science Association's Information Technology and Politics section and is associate editor for political science for the *Social Science Computer Review*. He is the project director for the Illinois State and Illinois Wesleyan Universities' Habitat for Humanity Collegiate Home.